best | designed

Jons Messedat

flagship stores

SHOPS . SHOWROOMS . BRAND CENTERS
GESCHÄFTE . SHOWROOMS . MARKENWELTEN

avedition

content

introduction | space meets brand

Brands are now the most valuable assets on the global market. The roof of a strong and credible brand offers both protection and identity to its suppliers and customers. They strongly influence our public spaces and the culture of everyday life as crowd-pleasers through their presence. We let ourselves be entertained, seduced, and sometimes even blinded by brands and their images. A transformation in the communication of brand images has occurred in recent times. To assert themselves on the international market, companies are increasingly presenting

their products within their own architectural framework. Direct advertising no longer stands in the forefront but rather the idea, the lifestyle, and the attitude that a product portrays. These are precisely the qualities that are concentrated in a distinct place so that customers and visitors can experience the authentic essence of the brand. Flagship stores, showrooms, and brand environments are scenographically designed places that awaken emotions, acquire sympathy, and publicly prove expertise. In this process, the uniform corporate design is no longer in

the forefront but the goal of creating a unique and distinctive business location. As lively places that appeal to all of the senses, they stand up to the anonymous periphery and the virtual spaces of the internet in the long run. Milestones in this development such as the Olivetti showrooms from the mid-20th Century belong to the avant-garde of architecture and design. A new building challenge has emerged, developing into a dynamic trendsetter of contemporary corporate architecture.

Flagship stores are primarily built at first-class and highly frequented locations of large international cities This is where an individual manufacturer usually offers the entire range of products or the complete service package in an upmarket spatial environment. Showrooms are the representatives of brands that stage the products and company philosophies throughout the world. Brand environments convey more about the background of a brand. They are often closely connected with tradition at the historically evolved location and complement the developed production sites with documentary and museum functions. The transitions between the individual presentation forms are fluid. What they all have in common is the ambition to not just characterize a company in the sense of "branding" but also to actively get to know it on the site. A great variety of companies make their brand the focus of a spatial staging with the goal of creating an emotional connection between the manufacturer and the customer. The spectrum extends from fashion and sporting articles to luxury goods and the products that surround us in our private ambience to the providers of modern communication technology. This book presents a selection of remarkable solutions from various fields that show the current approaches and visionary tendencies for this exciting and innovative task.

Jons Messedat

introduction | begegnung von raum und marke

Marken sind heute die kostbarsten Güter im globalen Markt. Das Dach einer starken und glaubwürdigen Marke bietet gleichermaßen Schutz und Identität für Anbieter und Kunden. Marken sind aber auch Publikumsmagneten, die durch ihre Präsenz unsere öffentlichen Räume und die heutige Alltagskultur prägen. Wir lassen uns von Marken und den Bildern, die sie uns vermitteln, unterhalten, verführen und manchmal sogar blenden. In jüngster Zeit findet ein Wandel in der Kommunikation von Markenbildern statt. Um sich auf dem internationalen Markt zu behaupten, prä-

sentieren Unternehmen ihre Marken immer häufiger in einem eigenen architektonischen Rahmen. Hier steht nicht mehr die direkte Werbung für das Produkt im Vordergrund, sondern die Idee, der Lebensstil und die Haltung, die es verkörpert. Genau diese Eigenschaften werden an einem unverwechselbaren Ort konzentriert, damit Kunden und Besucher den authentischen Markenkern erleben können. Flagship-Stores, Showrooms und Markenwelten sind szenografisch gestaltete Orte, an denen Emotionen geweckt, Sympathie gewonnen und Kompetenzen öffentlich bewiesen

werden. Dabei steht nicht mehr das einheitliche Corporate Design im Vordergrund, sondern das Ziel, eine einzigartige und unverwechselbare Adresse zu schaffen. Als lebendige Orte, die alle Sinne ansprechen, bieten sie der anonymen Peripherie und den virtuellen Räumen des Internet langfristig Paroli. Meilensteine in dieser Entwicklung, wie beispielsweise die Olivetti-Showrooms aus der Mitte des vergangenen Jahrhunderts gehören zur Avantgarde von Architektur und Design. Es ist eine neue Bauaufgabe entstanden, die sich zu einem rasanten Pulsgeber der zeit-

genössischen Corporate Architecture entwickelt hat. Flagship-Stores entstehen vor allem an erstklassigen und stark frequentierten Adressen der internationalen Metropolen. Hier wird meistens die gesamte Produktpalette oder das komplette Servicepaket eines einzelnen Herstellers in einem anspruchsvollen räumlichen Umfeld angeboten. Showrooms sind Repräsentanzen von Marken, in denen Produkte und Unternehmensinhalte weltweit inszeniert werden. Markenwelten dienen dazu, mehr über den Hintergrund einer Marke zu vermitteln. Oft sind sie eng mit der Tradition am

historisch gewachsenen Standort verbunden und ergänzen die gewachsenen Produktionsstätten mit dokumentarischen und musealen Funktionen. Die Übergänge zwischen den einzelnen Präsentationsformen sind fließend. Allen gemeinsam ist das Bestreben, ein Unternehmen nicht nur im Sinne des „Brandings" zu kennzeichnen, sondern es vor Ort aktiv kennenzulernen. Unternehmen aus den unterschiedlichsten Bereichen machen ihre Marke zum Mittelpunkt einer räumlichen Inszenierung mit dem Ziel, eine emotionale Bindung zwischen Hersteller und Kunde herzu-

stellen. Die Bandbreite reicht von Herstellern aus dem Bereich von Mode- und Sportartikeln sowie Luxusgütern und Dingen, die uns im privaten Ambiente umgeben, bis hin zu Anbietern aus der modernen Kommunikationstechnologie. In diesem Buch wird eine Auswahl von bemerkenswerten Lösungen aus ganz verschiedenen Branchen präsentiert, die aktuelle Ansätze und visionäre Tendenzen für diese spannende und innovative Aufgabenstellung aufzeigen.

Jons Messedat

fashion . sports

adidas originals store | new york . usa
DESIGN: EOOS

New York is the native town of the adidas Originals collection because it is where the sneakers and jackets of the 1950s and 1960s were rediscovered and introduced to the club scene through flea markets. The Originals Store in SoHo takes up this legend and translates it into modern terms. Its origin is the anonymous street market where the articles of yesterday are transformed into the trends of tomorrow. The vision of the EOOS designers was to define a shop without the cult of surfaces and architecture. The merchandise is exhibited, tried on, and purchased in a place that has no fixed installations. The assortment is presented on large tables. The mobile wall elements have merchandise attached to them with magnets and no visible supporting structure. The Originals store in SoHo is especially close to the original concept of the street market because it is housed in a former garage. The door can be raised and the customer enters the salesroom without having to step over a threshold. The concept of the Originals Stores has been realized almost 60 times throughout the world since 2001. The company founder and man for whom it was named, Adi Dassler, already used the insignia of the adidas brand – the characteristic three parallel stripes – on his first handmade sneakers.

New York ist die Geburtsstadt der adidas Originals Kollektion, denn dort wurden die Sportschuhe und Jacken der 50er und 60er Jahre wiederentdeckt und über Flohmärkte in die Klubszene eingeführt. Der Originals Store in SoHo nimmt diesen Mythos auf und setzt ihn zeitgemäß um. Der Ursprung ist der anonyme Straßenmarkt, wo sich Artikel von gestern in die Trends von morgen verwandeln. Die Vision der Designer von EOOS war es, einen Shop ohne den Kult von Oberflächen und Architektur zu definieren. Das Ausstellen, Anprobieren und Kaufen findet an einem Ort statt, es gibt keine festen Einbauten, und das Angebot wird auf großformatigen Tischen präsentiert. An den mobilen Wandelementen sind die Waren ohne eine sichtbare Tragstruktur mit Magneten befestigt. Der Originals Store in SoHo kommt der Idee des ursprünglichen Konzeptes des Straßenmarktes besonders nahe, da er in einer ehemaligen Garage untergebracht ist. Das Tor kann hochgefahren werden, und der Kunde betritt den Verkaufsraum ohne eine Schwelle zu überwinden. Das Konzept der Originals Stores wurde seit 2001 fast 60-mal weltweit umgesetzt. Das Erkennungszeichen der Marke adidas, die typischen drei parallelen Streifen, hat der Firmengründer und Namensgeber Adi Dassler bereits auf seinen ersten handgefertigten Turnschuhen verwendet.

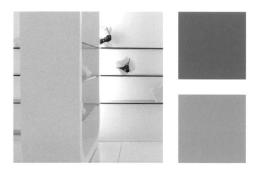

bizarre | omaha . usa
DESIGN: Randy Brown Architects

Good ideas are sometimes created on paper or through the folding of paper, as in the case of the Bizarre store that opened in 2005 in Omaha, Nebraska. During the design process, architect Randy Brown had cut into a piece of paper, bent the remaining strips, and formed a continuous space model. The result in the scale of 1:1 is surprising and just as consistent as the paper model. The elements of the interior such as the floor, walls, ceiling, and furnishings form a homogeneous structure. The salesroom focuses on the merchandise, which is presented on glass bases in U-shaped shelves. All of the sculptural installations such as sales counters, shelves, and wall elements received a white coat of paint. The highly polished – also white – synthetic resin floor further intensifies the immaterial effect. The indirect lighting supports the puristic aura of the space and also attracts attention beyond the store window. Deep views and outlooks through the transparent shelves allow the boundary between inside and outside to blur. A curved canopy appears to break through the facade and makes a prominent statement in the street spaces for this store, which itself is somewhat "bizarre".

Manchmal entstehen gute Ideen auf dem Papier oder durch die Faltung von Papier, wie im Falle des 2005 eröffneten Bizarre Stores in Omaha, Nebraska. Der Architekt Randy Brown hat während des Entwurfsprozesses ein Blatt Papier eingeschnitten, die verbleibenden Stege gebogen und daraus ein kontinuierliches Raummodell geformt. Das Ergebnis im Maßstab 1:1 überrascht und ist ebenso konsequent wie das Papiermodell. Die Elemente des Innenraumes wie Boden, Wände, Decke und die Möblierung bilden eine homogene Struktur. Im Mittelpunkt des Verkaufsraumes steht die Ware, die auf Glasböden in U-förmigen Regalen präsentiert wird. Alle skulpturalen Einbauten wie Verkaufstresen, Regale und Wandelemente erhielten einen weißen Anstrich. Der hochglänzende, ebenfalls weiße Kunstharzboden verstärkt die immaterielle Wirkung zusätzlich. Die indirekte Beleuchtung unterstützt die puristische Aura des Raumes und sorgt für Aufmerksamkeit auch jenseits des Schaufensters. Tiefe Ein- und Ausblicke durch die transparenten Regale hindurch lassen die Grenze von Innen und Außen verschwimmen. Ein geschwungenes Vordach scheint die Fassade zu durchbrechen und setzt ein markantes Zeichen im Straßenraum für diesen selbst etwas „bizarren" Store.

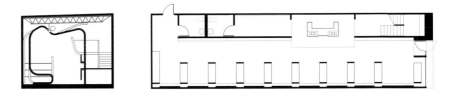

hugo boss flagship store | shanghai . china

DESIGN: Blocher Blocher Partners, Graphicdesign: Alan Chan Design

The new flagship store of Hugo Boss in Shanghai opened in 2006 on the Bund, which is the name for the historical promenade along the Huangpu River. The Bund offers an impressive view of the modern skyline and – as one of the last founding-era quarters – documents the significance of the city during the colonial period. Today an ever-increasing number of international brands are setting up extravagant stores in these buildings, some of which are listed on a historical register. In addition to the brand philosophy, the architects of Blocher Blocher Partners have also incorporated local structural conditions and aspects of the regional culture into the planning in collaboration with Alan Chan Design, Hong Kong. The interior design explores the overlapping of tradition and modern brand message, mediating between the cultures. As a result, the black-and-red varnished, highly polished cubes pay tribute to the tradition of the country. In the department for men's clothing, a wall of mirrors with historical motifs on the Bund creates the background for the current merchandise presentation. The materials and variation of design elements serve to define the individual areas of the room, which is more than 20 feet tall. For example, the slate in the Menswear Department is used in an uneven form while it is polished smooth in the area of Womanswear.

Der neue Flagship-Store von Hugo Boss in Shanghai eröffnete 2006 am Bund, wie die historische Uferpromenade am Huangpu-Fluss genannt wird. Der Bund bietet eine beeindruckende Aussicht auf die Kulisse der modernen Skyline und dokumentiert als eines der letzten Gründerzeitviertel die Bedeutung der Stadt zur Kolonialzeit. Heute lassen sich in den teilweise denkmalgeschützten Gebäuden immer mehr internationale Marken mit aufwändigen Stores nieder. Die Architekten von Blocher Blocher Partners, Stuttgart, haben neben der Markenphilosophie auch die lokalen Gegebenheiten und Aspekte der regionalen Kultur in Zusammenarbeit mit Alan Chan Design, Hongkong, in die Planungen einfließen lassen. Die Innenraumgestaltung thematisiert die Überlagerung von Tradition und moderner Markenbotschaft und vermittelt zwischen den Kulturen. So zollen die schwarz und rot lackierten, hochglänzenden Kuben ein Tribut an die Tradition des Landes. In der Abteilung für Männerbekleidung bildet eine Spiegelwand mit historischen Motiven zum Bund den Hintergrund für die aktuelle Warenpräsentation. Die verwendeten Materialien und die Variation der Gestaltungselemente dienen der Abgrenzung der einzelnen Bereiche in dem über sechs Meter hohen Raum. So wird zum Beispiel der Schiefer in der Menswear Abteilung spaltrau verwendet, während er im Bereich Womanswear glatt geschliffen zum Einsatz kommt.

eliden, lotte department store | seoul . korea
DESIGN: Universal Design Studio Ltd.

In the luxury department store Lotte, located at the center of the South Korean metropolis of Seoul, various design labels have presented themselves on a total area of more than 3,000 square feet since 2005. The challenge for Universal Design Studio Ltd. of London was to define a mutual framework for the 20 premium-segment suppliers of clothing and accessories that differentiates the large area but doesn't divide it. In order to achieve this, the architects integrated two levels into the existing selling area to structure the space. The various stores are connected by a wall measuring 164 feet and covered with three-dimensional ceramic tiles. The abstracted flower ornamentation was inspired by traditional patterns that are firmly anchored in the Korean religion and everyday life. The second level of organization is a net structure that splits the individual areas of the space into separate but transparent zones. Different variations in an array of sizes and materials were developed for these partitions, with a spectrum ranging from white printed glass to elements of massive black varnished wood. Because it transformed traditional elements into contemporary design, Eliden has succeeded in being perceived as an independent brand.

Im Luxus-Kaufhaus Lotte, mitten in der südkoreanischen Metropole Seoul, präsentieren sich seit 2005 verschiedene Design-Labels auf einer Gesamtfläche von mehr als 1 000 Quadratmetern. Die Herausforderung für Universal Design Studio Ltd. aus London war es, für die 20 Anbieter von Kleidung und Accessoires aus dem Premiumsegment einen gemeinsamen Rahmen zu definieren, der den großzügigen Raum differenziert, aber nicht unterteilt. Um dies zu erreichen, integrierten die Architekten zwei Ebenen zur Raumgliederung in die bestehende Verkaufsfläche. Eine 50 Meter lange Wand, mit einer dreidimensionalen Keramikfliese verkleidet, verbindet die unterschiedlichen Geschäfte. Das abstrahierte Blumenornament ist von traditionellen Mustern inspiriert, die fest in der koreanischen Religion und im Alltag verankert sind. Die zweite Gliederungsebene ist eine Netzstruktur, die einzelne Raumbereiche in separate aber transparente Zonen abgrenzt. Für diese Raumteiler wurden verschiedene Varianten in unterschiedlichen Maßstäben und Materialien entwickelt. Die Bandbreite reicht von weiß bedrucktem Glas bis hin zu Elementen aus massivem, schwarz lackiertem Holz. Mit der zeitgemäßen Transformation von traditionellen Elementen ist es gelungen, dass Eliden heute als eigenständige Marke wahrgenommen wird.

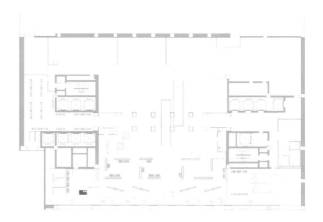

falke flagship store | berlin . germany

DESIGN: Keggenhoff | Partner

Opened in April 2006, the flagship store represents a clear commitment to the location of Berlin. Directly on the Kurfürstendamm, the company – which was founded in 1895 as a sock manufacturer – highlights values such as tradition, quality, and an awareness of trends. The architects Keggenhoff und Partner translated the guiding principles of dynamics and urbanity into a system of independent surfaces and formats. The alternation between open and closed spaces, as well as vertical and horizontal levels with projections and offsets, looks like 3-D graphic art. The product itself becomes a part of this user interface that can be experienced both optically and tactually. For example, customers can look at colors directly next to each other and feel the various fabric qualities. The presentation is composed of three levels leading from one to the next in the Walk of Style. The foreground displays product information, and the background extensively stages a theme related to the city of Berlin. There is room between them for the products, which are presented in a linear way and in different variations. Space has been created here not only for products of the basic assortment, but also for collections and luxury articles that vary depending on the season.

Der im April 2006 eröffnete Flagship-Store bedeutet für FALKE ein klares Bekenntnis zum Standort Berlin. Unmittelbar am Kurfürstendamm setzt das 1895 als Strumpfmanufaktur gegründete Unternehmen Werte wie Tradition, Qualität und Trendbewusstsein in Szene. Die Architekten Keggenhoff und Partner übersetzten die Leitgedanken Dynamik und Urbanität in ein System aus unabhängigen Flächen und Formaten. Der Wechsel von offenen und geschlossenen Flächen sowie von vertikalen und horizontalen Ebenen mit Vor- und Rücksprüngen wirkt wie eine dreidimensionale Grafik. Das Produkt selbst wird zu einem Teil dieser optisch und haptisch erlebbaren Benutzeroberfläche. So können die Kunden beispielsweise Farben direkt nebeneinander betrachten und verschiedene Stoffqualitäten fühlen. Die Präsentation setzt sich aus drei hintereinander geschalteten Ebenen am sogenannten „Walk of Style" zusammen. Im Vordergrund steht die Information zum Produkt, im Hintergrund ist jeweils ein Thema zum Standort Berlin großflächig inszeniert. Dazwischen ist Platz für die Produkte, die linear und in verschiedenen Varianten präsentiert werden. Hier wurde nicht nur Raum für die Produkte des Basis-Sortiments geschaffen, sondern auch für saisonal unterschiedliche Kollektionen und Luxusartikel.

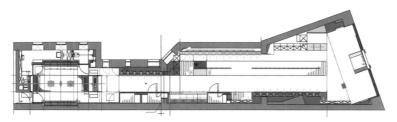

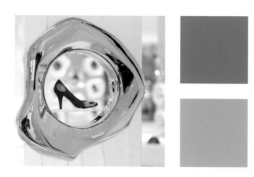

fornarina | las vegas . usa
DESIGN: giorgio borruso design

Rhodamine Red is the signature color of the Italian fashion label Fornarina, which was launched in the American gambling and entertainment paradise of Las Vegas with an unusual flagship store. While the previous stores have been strongly influenced by the characteristic company color, only small accents of it can be found in Las Vegas. The California-based Italian architect Giorgio Borruso selected a neutral color background to create a counterpart to the artificial metropolis in which the day and night architecture stand in spectacular competition with each other. In 1947, Gianfranco Fornarini founded the fashion label Fornarina in Italy. After the company had made a name for itself with extravagant women's shoes, the collection was expanded to include clothing and accessories some years ago. The prototype for a new generation of Fornarina shops opened in February 2004. In the interior of the flagship store, four huge lighting fixtures of organically formed fabric membrane were suspended from the ceiling and emphasize the free area at the center of the room. The large fiberglass sculptural pieces that cover the walls pick up the theme of the organic forms, as do the ring-shaped elements for the presentation of shoes and smaller accessories. This has created an independent inner world that attracts attention even in Las Vegas.

Rhodamin ist die charakteristische Farbe des italienischen Modelabels Fornarina, das im amerikanischen Spieler- und Vergnügungsparadies Las Vegas mit einem außergewöhnlichen Flagship-Store an den Start ging. Während die bisherigen Geschäfte stark durch die charakteristische Hausfarbe geprägt sind, findet man in Las Vegas nur kleinere Akzente davon. Der aus Kalifornien stammende italienische Architekt Giorgio Borruso hat einen farblich neutralen Hintergrund gewählt, um einen Gegenpol zu der künstlichen Metropole zu schaffen, in der sich Tag- und Nachtarchitektur spektakuläre Schaukämpfe leisten. Gianfranco Fornarini gründete 1947 das Modelabel Fornarina in Italien. Nachdem das Unternehmen sich mit extravaganten Damenschuhen einen Namen gemacht hatte, wurde die Kollektion vor einigen Jahren durch Bekleidung und Accessoires ergänzt. Der Prototyp für eine neue Generation von Fornarina Shops eröffnete im Februar 2004. Im Innenraum des Flagship-Stores wurden vier überdimensionale Beleuchtungskörper aus organisch geformten Stoffmembranen von der Decke abgehängt, die den freien Platz in der Raummitte betonen. Die großen Wandverkleidungen aus Fiberglas nehmen das Thema der organischen Formen ebenso auf wie die ringförmigen Elemente zur Präsentation von Schuhen und kleineren Accessoires. Es ist eine eigenständige Innenwelt entstanden, die sogar in Las Vegas für Aufsehen sorgt.

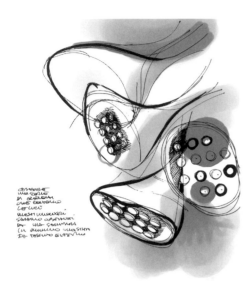

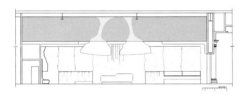

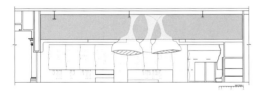

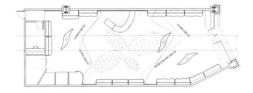

humanic store | vienna . austria

DESIGN: Hans Michael Heger, Humanic Design

The stores of the Humanic shoe brand initially make an impression due to their size. Following the megastore in Cologne with almost 11,500 square feet of selling space, the company opened two more locations in Vienna in rapid succession. The concept of the company's stores with its spacious outlets clearly stands out from the competition in the heavily frequented downtown areas. Instead of a uniform appearance, each store is unique and prefers to preserve traces of existing building substance. Although the interior design vocabulary follows the same patterns, it does not appear to be a regimented system. The Humanic flagship store is situated in an old building from the late 19th Century in the Mariahilferstrasse pedestrian shopping district. Very little substance remained of the original size and design of the business premises after several renovations. The heavy wood paneling was contrasted with new colors and materials that create a contemporary and friendly background for the presentation of merchandise. The cream-colored floors also contribute to this impression, together with the use of pastel green. The dramaturgical placement of lighting creates differentiated accents on the presentation tables. The illuminated display cases and feature walls are adapted to the changing seasons.

Die Stores der Schuhmarke Humanic beeindrucken zunächst durch ihre Größe. Nach dem Megastore in Köln mit 3 500 Quadratmetern Verkaufsfläche eröffnete das Unternehmen 2005 in rascher Folge zwei weitere Geschäfte in Wien. Das Konzept der Stores des Unternehmens hebt sich mit den großzügigen Filialen in stark frequentierten Innenstadtlagen deutlich von der Konkurrenz ab. Es wird kein einheitliches Erscheinungsbild angestrebt, sondern jeder Store ist ein Unikat, das auch gerne Spuren der vorgefundenen Bausubstanz erhält. Das Vokabular der Innenarchitektur folgt zwar gleichen Mustern, aber es kommt nicht der Eindruck eines reglementierten Systems auf. Der Flagship-Store Humanic befindet sich in einem Altbau aus der Gründerzeit in der Einkaufsmeile Mariahilferstraße. Von der ursprünglichen Größe und Ausstattung der Geschäftsräume war nach mehreren Umbauten nicht mehr viel Substanz vorhanden. Der wuchtigen Holzvertäfelung wurden neue Farben und Materialien entgegengesetzt, die einen zeitgemäßen und freundlichen Hintergrund für die Präsentation der Waren bilden. Der cremefarbene Boden trägt dazu ebenso bei wie die Verwendung von zartem Grün. Die dramaturgische Lichtführung setzt differenzierte Akzente auf den Präsentationstischen, leuchtende Vitrinen und Featurewände passen sich dem saisonalen Wechsel an.

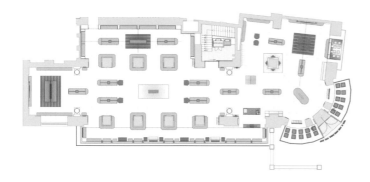

carlos miele flagship store | new york . usa

DESIGN: Asymptote

The flagship store of the Brazilian fashion designer Carlos Miele opened in June 2003 in the prosperous New York Meatpacking District. This is where the Brazilian attitude toward life and South American culture meet the cool precision of cutting-edge technologies and production engineering. This is reflected in both the clothing by Carlos Miele and the architecture by Hani Rashid and Lise Anne Couture of Asymptote's New York office. The interior of the store is a spacious white room with a subtle palette of colors that shows traces of pale green and nuances of blue and gray. The restrained color scheme provides a neutral background for the expressive and highly colorful designs by Carlos Miele. The center of the store is marked by a sculpture that stretches from the floor to the ceiling and meanders through the entire length of the interior. The organic use of form creates places to sit, as well as niches for the presentation of merchandise. Just like the fashion designer's products, the entire module was made according to CAD layouts and prefabricated outside of the store. As a whole, the spatial ambience appears to be an artistic intervention within the metropolis that possesses a trans-urban mixture of Sao Paulo and New York city cultures.

Im prosperierenden New Yorker Meatpacking District eröffnete im Juni 2003 der Flagship-Store des brasilianischen Modedesigners Carlos Miele. Hier treffen brasilianisches Lebensgefühl und südamerikanische Kultur auf die kühle Präzision modernster Technologien und Fertigungstechniken. Dies spiegelt sich sowohl in den Kleidungsstücken von Carlos Miele als auch in der Architektur des New Yorker Büros Asymptote von Hani Rashid und Lise Anne Couture wider. Das Innere des Stores ist ein großzügiger weißer Raum mit einer dezenten Farbpalette, die Spuren von blassem Grün sowie blaue und graue Nuancen aufweist. Die zurückhaltende Farbgebung bildet einen neutralen Hintergrund für die expressiven und stark farbigen Entwürfe von Carlos Miele. Den Mittelpunkt des Geschäftes markiert eine Skulptur, die sich vom Boden bis zur Decke erstreckt und durch die gesamte Länge des Innenraumes mäandert. Die organische Formensprache schafft sowohl Sitzgelegenheiten als auch Nischen zur Präsentation der Waren. Das gesamte Element wurde ähnlich wie die Produkte des Modedesigners nach CAD Zuschnitten gefertigt und außerhalb des Ladens vorgefertigt. Insgesamt erscheint das räumliche Ambiente wie eine künstlerische Intervention im Stadtraum, mit einer „trans-urbanen" Mischung der Stadtkulturen von Sao Paulo und New York.

nike air jordan xxperience | denver . usa

DESIGN: Skylab Design Group

With its Niketown concept, which has been developed and implemented throughout the world since the 1990s, Nike is among the trailblazers of the flagship store idea. To celebrate the market launch of the 20th Nike Air Jordan shoe, the company installed a temporary showroom in an empty loft in Denver, Colorado under the motto of "2005 Jordan XXperience". During the NBA Allstar Weekend in February 2005, the public area was transformed into an exclusive VIP lounge every evening. Many motifs with the most important stages of basketball legend Michael Jordan's career are illustrated on the new basketball-and-lifestyle shoe, the design of which is oriented upon motorcycling. These elements became the main motifs of the production, which was developed by the designers and architects of the Skylab Design Group from Portland, Oregon. They divided the presentation area into an exhibition and an interactive zone. The narrow exhibit area is designed like the exhaust pipe of a motorcycle. Its walls hold showcases and displays, behind which motorcycles have been positioned. The nearly 100-foot long interactive zone offers visitors additional attractions such as a gaming pod, a music pod, and a comfortable lounge.

Nike gehört mit dem Niketown-Konzept, das seit den 90er Jahren entwickelt und weltweit realisiert wird, zu den Vorreitern der Flagship-Store Idee. Anlässlich der Markteinführung des 20. „Nike Air Jordan"-Schuhs, installierte das Unternehmen in einem leer stehenden Loft in Denver in Colorado einen temporären Showroom unter dem Motto „2005 Jordan XXperience". Während des NBA Allstar Wochenendes im Februar 2005 verwandelte sich der öffentliche Bereich allabendlich in eine exklusive VIP-Lounge. Zahlreiche Motive mit den wichtigsten Stationen aus der Karriere der Basketballlegende Michael Jordan finden sich an dem neuen Basketball- und Lifestyle-Schuh, dessen Design sich an den Motorradsport anlehnt. Diese Elemente wurden zum zentralen Motiv der Inszenierung, welche die Designer und Architekten der Skylab Design Group aus Portland in Oregon gestalteten. Sie teilten die Präsentationsfläche in eine Ausstellungs- und in eine Erlebniszone auf. Der schmale Ausstellungsbereich gestaltet sich wie ein Motorradauspuff, an dessen Wänden sich Vitrinen und Displays befinden, hinter denen Motorräder platziert wurden. In der 30 Meter langen Erlebniszone warteten zusätzliche Attraktionen wie beispielsweise ein „gaming pod", ein „music pod" und eine komfortable Lounge auf die Besucher.

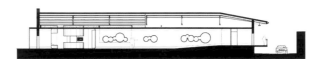

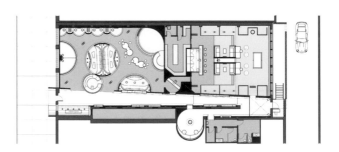

puma flagship store | prague . czech republic

DESIGN: moysig retail design gmbh

The marketing activities by PUMA have recently aimed at the merging of sports and fashion to make the brand the epitome of the "sports lifestyle". The cooperation with the Hamburg fashion designer Jil Sander at the end of the 1990s was a milestone on this path. It was followed by the collaboration with many outstanding designers such as Philippe Starck. At the same time, PUMA has sponsored top teams and athletes time and again and included them in its brand campaigns since their qualities like spontaneity, authenticity, and individuality correspond with the values of the company. The area of retail is an important component in the company's strategy. In 1999, the first concept store opened in Santa Monica, California, and the brand is now represented with shops throughout the world. PUMA opened a store in Chodov, a suburb of Prague, at one of the largest shopping centers of Europe in November 2005. The clear and recognizable store concept ensures that customers can find their way in the familiar ambience no matter where they are. Above all, it appeals to young customers and informs them about product innovations. As a result, the company intensifies customer loyalty and learns more about their desires and needs in order to base future developements upon them.

Die Marketingaktivitäten von PUMA zielen in jüngster Zeit auf die Verschmelzung von Sport und Mode ab, um die Marke zum Inbegriff von „Sportlifestyle" zu machen. Einen Meilenstein auf dem Weg dorthin bedeutete Ende der 90er Jahre die Kooperation mit der hanseatischen Modedesignerin Jil Sander. Es folgte die Zusammenarbeit mit zahlreichen herausragenden Designern wie etwa Philippe Starck. Gleichzeitig fördert PUMA immer wieder Spitzenteams und Athleten und bezieht sie in die Markenkampagnen ein, da sich die Eigenschaften der Sportler wie Spontaneität, Authentizität und Individualität mit den Werten des Unternehmens decken. Der Bereich Retail ist ein wichtiger Baustein in der Unternehmensstrategie. 1999 wurde der erste Konzept Store in Santa Monica in Kalifornien eröffnet, und mittlerweile ist die Marke weltweit mit Shops vertreten. Im November 2005 eröffnete PUMA einen Store in Chodov, einem Vorort von Prag, in einem der größten Einkaufszentren Europas. Das klare und wiedererkennbare Store-Konzept sorgt dafür, dass sich der Kunde überall im vertrauten Ambiente wiederfindet. Es spricht vor allem junge Käufer an und informiert sie über Produktinnovationen. Das Unternehmen vertieft damit die Kundenbindung und erfährt mehr über die Wünsche und Bedürfnisse der Käufer, um zukünftige Entwicklungen daran auszurichten.

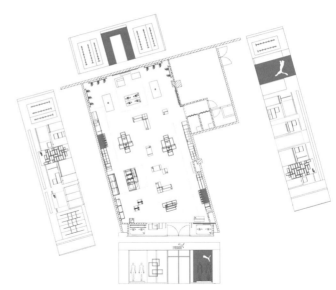

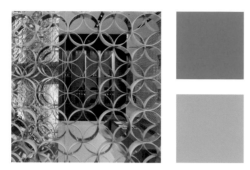

louis vuitton | tokyo, roppongi hills . japan

DESIGN: Louis Vuitton Architecture Department, Jun Aoki and Aurelio Clementi

As early as 1875, the trunk-maker Louis Vuitton accented the covering for his products with a recognizable pattern to set them apart from the competition. His idea of distinguishing all of the products with his own logo made him one of the forerunners of the many visibly embellished brand-name articles. The covering with a unique identity characterizes the product line and architecture of the stores belonging to this label, which is represented internationally. The company's own architecture department developed international shop concepts that are adapted to the respective city in collaboration with external architects. In Tokyo's Roppongi Hills district – which is primarily known for its nightlife – an additional flagship store was opened in September 2003. It was designed by Aurelio Clementi in collaboration with Jun Aoki and Eric Carlson of the Louis Vuitton architecture department. An oscillating honeycomb structure of Plexiglas tubes distinguishes the façade and causes a moiré effect. It is only possible to look directly into it from close up, and it offers a virtual impression from the distance. The interior is also dominated by honeycomb structures, which provide the background for the merchandise presentation. The boundaries between the architecture and the products become blurred.

Der Koffermacher Louis Vuitton versah schon im Jahre 1875 die Bespannung seiner Produkte mit einem wiedererkennbaren Muster, um sich gegenüber der Konkurrenz abzugrenzen. Mit seiner Idee, alle Produkte mit dem eigenen Logo zu kennzeichnen, wurde er zu einem der Vorläufer aller sichtbar gekennzeichneten Markenartikel. Die Umhüllung mit einer eigenen Identität prägt bis heute die Produktlinie und die Architektur der Geschäfte des weltweit vertretenen Labels. Die firmeninterne Architekturabteilung erarbeitete in Zusammenarbeit mit externen Architekten internationale Shop-Konzepte, die individuell auf den jeweiligen Ort abgestimmt sind. In Tokios Stadtteil Roppongi Hills, der vor allem durch sein Nachtleben bekannt ist, eröffnete im September 2003 ein weiterer Flagship-Store, den Aurelio Clementi in Zusammenarbeit mit Jun Aoki und Eric Carlson von der Louis Vuitton Architekturabteilung gestaltete. Eine oszillierende Wabenstruktur aus Plexiglasröhren prägt die Fassade, wodurch ein sogenannter Moiré-Effekt entsteht. Direkte Durchblicke sind nur aus der Nähe möglich, aus der Ferne bietet sich ein virtuell anmutender Eindruck. Auch im Innenraum dominieren wabenartige Strukturen, die den Hintergrund für die Warenpräsentation bieten. Die Grenzen zwischen Architektur und Produkten verschwimmen.

luxury . accessories

burri optik | zurich . switzerland

DESIGN: nimmrichter cda gmbh für architektur und kommunikationsdesign

Glasses are the main protagonists at the new flagship store of Burrioptik in the heart of Zurich. Located directly on the main artery of Uraniastrasse, the exterior effect of the optician store – which was remodeled in 2006 – is directed at both pedestrians and passing traffic. As a result, the extremely enlarged store windows allow a view of the many exhibits, which appear to float in space. The frames for the glasses are presented on transparent shelf bases that are distanced from the walls. The background illumination underscores the floating impression of the filigree construction and sheds the right light on more than 1 700 exhibits without letting the customer be overwhelmed by them. On the whole, the interior designed by Rolf Nimmrichter of Zurich appears to be an orderly, urbane gallery because of the exquisite and muted selection of materials. Dark Brazilian walnut wood contrasts with etched glass and the dyed concrete floor, which emanates an industrial character. The various consultation areas for sunglasses and optical glasses are clearly organized on the ground floor. The lower level has a studio and storerooms. The upper floor holds additional examination rooms.

Brillen sind die Hauptakteure im neuen Flagship-Store von Burrioptik im Herzen von Zürich. Unmittelbar an der stark befahrenen Uraniastraße gelegen, wurde die Außenwirkung des 2006 umgestalteten Optikergeschäftes nicht nur auf Passanten, sondern auch auf den fließenden Verkehr ausgerichtet. So geben die stark vergrößerten Schaufenster den Blick auf die zahlreichen Exponate frei, die im Raum zu schweben scheinen. Die Brillengestelle werden auf transparenten Regalböden präsentiert, die von den Wänden abgerückt sind. Die Hintergrundbeleuchtung unterstreicht den schwebenden Eindruck der filigranen Konstruktion und rückt die über 1 700 Exponate ins rechte Licht, ohne dass der Kunde den Überblick verliert. Insgesamt wirkt der von Rolf Nimmrichter aus Zürich gestaltete Innenraum durch eine edle und zurückhaltende Materialwahl wie eine aufgeräumte, urbane Galerie. Dunkles brasilianisches Nussbaumholz kontrastiert mit geätztem Glas und eingefärbtem Betonboden, der einen industriellen Charakter ausstrahlt. Die verschiedenen Beratungsbereiche für Sonnenbrillen und optische Brillen im Erdgeschoss sind klar gegliedert. Im Untergeschoss befinden sich Atelier und Lagerräume und im Obergeschoss weitere Untersuchungsräume.

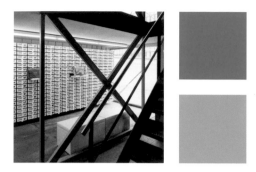

freitag lab. ag | zurich . switzerland

DESIGN: Search Architekten gmbh, Harald Echsle & Annette Spillmann architekten eth sia

In 1993, the brothers Markus und Daniel Freitag let themselves be inspired by the heavy truck traffic that rushed past their apartment on the Zurich road axis to make their first messenger bag out of old truck tarps, used bicycle inner tubes, and car seatbelts. This was the starting signal for the success story of the now legendary FREITAG bags. Because of strong expansion, the company had searched for an additional sales and presentation space close to the production site. They were offered a small lot between the road axis and the railroad tracks, which outstandingly suits the products made of used materials that are at home on the street. The Zurich architectural office of Harald Echsle & Annette Spillmann architekten set up a salesroom here in 17 used overseas containers that the Freitag brothers selected in Hamburg and had sent to Zurich on a freight train. These were stacked on top of each other at the site and connected through elements from the field of shipping. The tower of containers now forms a widely visible landmark between the international road axes. Using the same approach as for the bags made of truck tarps, the long walls and ceilings were removed. This has created a roomy interior space. Like its products, the Freitag flagship store – which was completed in 2006 – is an original made of recycled elements with a close relationship to traffic.

Die Brüder Markus und Daniel Freitag ließen sich 1993 vom Schwerverkehr, der unmittelbar an ihrer Wohnung an der Züricher Transitachse vorbeirauschte, für ihre erste Messenger Bag aus alten LKW-Planen, gebrauchten Fahrradschläuchen und Autositzgurten inspirieren. Dies war der Startschuss für die Erfolgsstory der mittlerweile legendären FREITAG Taschen. Aufgrund der starken Expansion suchte das Unternehmen nach einem zusätzlichen Verkaufs- und Präsentationsraum in der Nähe zur Produktionsstätte. Es bot sich ein kleines Grundstück zwischen Verkehrsachsen und Bahngleisen an, das hervorragend zu den Produkten aus gebrauchten Materialien passt, die auf der Straße zu Hause sind. Das Züricher Büro Harald Echsle & Annette Spillmann architekten richtete hier einen Verkaufsraum in 17 gebrauchten Überseecontainern ein, die die Freitag-Brüder in Hamburg aussuchten und per Bahn nach Zürich verfrachten ließen. Diese wurden vor Ort aufeinandergetürmt und mit Elementen aus der Schifffahrt miteinander verbunden. Der Turm aus Containern bildet nun eine weithin sichtbare Landmarke zwischen den internationalen Verkehrsachsen. Analog zu den Taschen aus LKW Planen wurden Längswände und Decken herausgetrennt und ein großzügiges Raumvolumen geschaffen. Der 2006 fertiggestellte Freitag Flagship-Store ist wie die Produkte ein Unikat aus wieder verwendeten Elementen mit engem Bezug zum Verkehr.

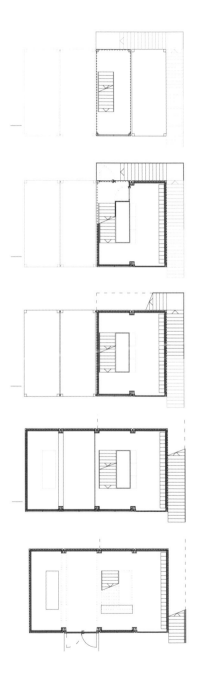

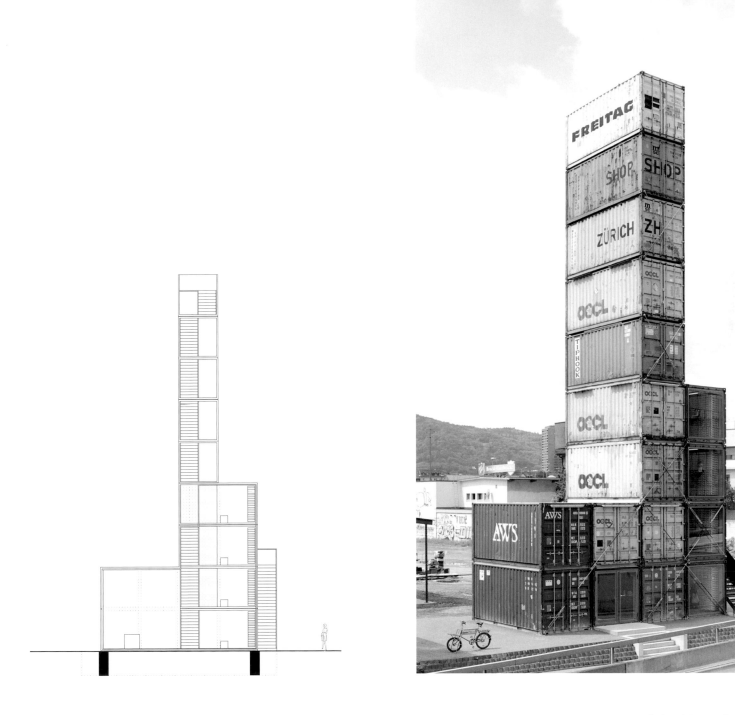

montblanc | tokyo . japan

DESIGN: Andreas Weidner, Montblanc International GmbH with Kerstin Bartram, Büro Bartram
based on Montblanc Boutique Concept of Jean-Michel Wilmotte, Paris

The Hamburg Montblanc company with its long-standing tradition has secured a solid place in the league of luxury-goods providers with its concept of "Timeless Luxury Crafted by the Mind." In October 2006, the new 1440 square-foot flagship boutique at the Montblanc Ginza Building opened in Tokyo's booming Ginza Chuo-dori district. The idea for the design is based upon the Montblanc boutique design concept that architect Jean-Michel Wilmotte created for the company in 2001. In collaboration with the Bartram office of Hamburg, interior designer Andreas Weidner of Montblanc International developed the adapted design and supervised its realization. Artistic quotations of Japanese culture and the puristic, clear use of form highlight the diversified range Montblanc of products, as well as the limited edition "Montblanc Ginza Honten", which was fashioned exclusively for this boutique. Female customers are offered jewelry, watches, leather goods, and writing implements on the ground floor while the second floor presents the classic masculine Montblanc assortment. The upper level has the customer service department, which allows insights into the Montblanc craftsmanship, and a VIP salon with a lounge and library where customers can relax with a view of the hustle and bustle on the street below.

Das Hamburger Traditionsunternehmen Montblanc hat sich mit dem Konzept „Timeless Luxury Crafted by the mind" einen festen Platz in der Liga der Anbieter von Luxusgütern gesichert. Im Oktober 2006 eröffnete in Tokio im boomenden Stadtteil Ginza Chuo-dori die neue 439 Quadratmeter große Flagship-Boutique im „The Montblanc Ginza Building". Die Entwurfsidee basiert auf dem Montblanc Boutique Design Konzept, das der Architekt Jean-Michel Wilmotte 2001 für Montblanc entwickelt hat. Der Interior Designer Andreas Weidner von Montblanc International hat in Zusammenarbeit mit dem Büro Bartram aus Hamburg sowohl das adaptierte Design entwickelt, als auch die Ausführung betreut. Gestalterische Zitate an die japanische Kultur und die puristische, klare Formensprache setzen die diversifizierte Montblanc Produktpalette sowie die exklusiv für diese Boutique entwickelten Limited Editions „Montblanc Ginza Honten" in Szene. Im Erdgeschoss werden den weiblichen Kunden Schmuck, Uhren, Lederwaren und Schreibgeräte angeboten, während in der ersten Etage das klassisch männliche Montblanc Sortiment präsentiert wird. Darüber befinden sich der Customer Service, der Einblick in die Montblanc Handwerkskunst gewährt, und ein VIP Salon mit Lounge und Bibliothek, in der man mit Blick auf das Treiben auf der Straße entspannen kann.

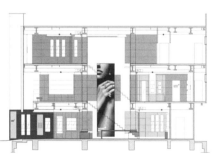

porsche design | berlin . germany
DESIGN: KMS, Matteo Thun

The Porsche Design Studio was established in 1972 by F.A. Porsche, designer of the automobile classic Porsche 911. During the past decades, it has primarily developed men's accessories such as watches, glasses, and writing implements. These are all sold under the parent brand of Porsche Design. A common factor for all of the designs is the clear, functional use of form and the combination of traditional craftsmanship with the cutting-edge technology. The core statement of the company – "Engineers of Luxury" – summarizes this attitude. The concept of the Porsche Design Stores was developed in order to present these values internationally in a suitable environment. In collaboration with the architect Matteo Thun and KMS, a store was created in Berlin that is oriented upon the basic principles of the products. As a result, the combination of natural and industrial materials also characterizes the interior. Dark oak and rough slate contrast with tinted glass and titanium-colored varnish. The "scantable" as the "gate to the future" is an expression of the most modern technology: If the customer places a product on the square block of slate, an integrated monitor and scanner record the surface. A matrix of all Porsche products appears on three performance walls, and it zooms in on the respective object. The screen of the scantable displays additional information about the product.

Das Porsche Design Studio wurde 1972 von F.A. Porsche, dem Designer des automobilen Klassikers Porsche 911, gegründet. In den vergangenen Jahrzehnten entstanden vor allem Herrenaccessoires wie beispielsweise Uhren, Brillen und Schreibgeräte, die unter dem Markendach „Porsche Design" vertrieben werden. Allen Entwürfen ist die klare, funktionale Formensprache und die Verbindung von handwerklicher Tradition mit modernster Technologie gemeinsam. Die Kernaussage des Unternehmens „Engineers of Luxury" fasst diese Haltung zusammen. Um diese Werte international in einem adäquaten Umfeld zu präsentieren, wurde das Konzept der Porsche Design Stores entwickelt. In Zusammenarbeit mit dem Architekten Matteo Thun und KMS wurde in Berlin ein Store realisiert, der sich an den Grundprinzipien der Produkte orientiert. So prägt die Kombination von natürlichen und industriellen Materialien auch den Innenraum. Dunkles Eichenholz und rauer Schiefer kontrastieren mit getöntem Glas und titanfarbenem Lack. Der „Scantable" als „Gate to the Future" ist Ausdruck modernster Technologie: Legt der Kunde ein Produkt auf den quadratischen Schieferblock, erfassen ein integrierter Monitor und Scanner die Oberfläche. Auf drei bespielten Wänden erscheint eine Matrix aller Porsche Produkte, und das entsprechende Objekt wird herangezoomt. Der Bildschirm des Scantable zeigt weitere Informationen zu dem Produkt.

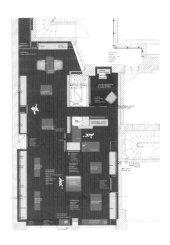

swarovski | prague . czech republic

DESIGN: internally developed store design concept

The Austrian company Swarovski is famous for the production of jewelry and accessories of cut crystal. The company invites visitors on an exciting journey of discovery through the crystal world of Swarovski at the company headquarters in Wattens, Tyrol. The family business has gradually diversified the product range and now sells it internationally. The company's own stores form the interface with the customers and the architectural framework for the glamorous presentations of the products. Founder Daniel Swarovski I originally came from Bohemia, where he revolutionized the crystal industry with the invention of a new machine for crystal-cutting. So it was a special obligation for the company to show its presence in Prague with a representative flagship store. A branch had already been there since 2002, but this was considerably expanded after it moved. The new store, which opened in September 2006, is in the best location and has a floorspace of about 1,300 square feet. The name of the company and the family sparkles in large letters above the entrance. In the interior of the store – which was designed by the company itself – curtains of individual crystals form the glittering background for products that also sparkle as they are displayed in their classic showcases.

Das österreichische Unternehmen Swarovski ist bekannt für die Produktion von Schmuck und Accessoires aus geschliffenem Kristall. Am Stammsitz in Wattens in Tirol lädt das Unternehmen zu einer spannenden Entdeckungsreise durch die Swarovski-Kristallwelten ein. Das Familienunternehmen hat die Produktpalette sukzessiv diversifiziert und vertreibt sie heute weltweit. Firmeneigene Geschäfte bilden die Schnittstelle zum Kunden und den architektonischen Rahmen für die glamouröse Inszenierung der Produkte. Der Gründer Daniel Swarovski I. stammte ursprünglich aus Böhmen, wo er die Kristallindustrie mit der Erfindung einer neuen Maschine für den Kristallschliff revolutionierte. So war es für das Unternehmen eine besondere Verpflichtung, in Prag mit einem repräsentativen Flagship-Store Präsenz zu zeigen. Das Unternehmen führte dort bereits seit 2002 eine Filiale, die sich durch einen Umzug wesentlich vergrößerte. Der im September 2006 eröffnete Store befindet sich in bester Lage und verfügt über eine Fläche von fast 400 Quadratmetern. Über dem Eingang prangt der Firmen- und Familienname in großen Lettern. Im Inneren des firmenintern gestalteten Ladens bilden Vorhänge aus Einzelkristallen den glitzernden Hintergrund für die ebenso funkelnden Produkte, die in klassischen Vitrinen präsentiert werden.

home . living

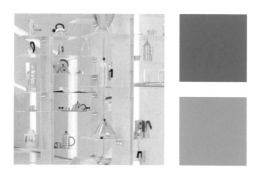

alessi | new york, soho . usa

DESIGN: Asymptote

The Alessi family has been producing metalware for generations at Lake Orta in northern Italy. From here, Alberto Alessi's ancestors traveled in all directions to learn the craft of tinsmithing. Silver, aluminum, and - most recently - stainless steel are other materials that have been added over time. Since the 1980s, the company has worked with famous designers and architects such as Aldo Rossi, Alessandro Mendini, Ettore Sottsass, Michael Graves, Enzo Mari, and Richard Sapper – just to name a few. The award-winning products have influenced the contemporary history of design and are distributed throughout the world. In the course of a basic image adjustment, the firm employed the New York office of Asymptote to create additional products, construct an innovative corporate design, and draw up plans for the new flagship store. The store, which opened in September 2006 in SoHo, displays a dynamic use of form that becomes possible through a close interlinking between digital designs and manufacturing processes. The architects developed a space that expresses a break from the formative influence of postmodernism and creates an appropriate framework for the presentation of products from a new generation of designers and architects.

Die Familie Alessi produziert bereits seit Generationen Metallwaren am oberitalienischen Ortasee. Die Vorfahren von Alberto Alessi gingen von dort aus in alle Richtungen, um das Handwerk des Zinngießens zu erlernen. Mit der Zeit kamen weitere Materialien wie Silber, Aluminium und schließlich Edelstahl hinzu. Seit den 80er Jahren arbeitet das Unternehmen mit namhaften Designern und Architekten wie Aldo Rossi, Alessandro Mendini, Ettore Sottsass, Michael Graves, Enzo Mari und Richard Sapper zusammen, um nur einige zu nennen. Die vielfach ausgezeichneten Produkte prägten die jüngere Designgeschichte und werden weltweit vertrieben. Im Zuge einer grundsätzlichen Überarbeitung des Erscheinungsbildes engagierte das Unternehmen das New Yorker Büro Asymptote, um neue Produkte, ein neues Corporate Design sowie den neuen Flagship-Store zu gestalten. Das im September 2006 in SoHo eröffnete Geschäft zeigt eine dynamische Formensprache, die durch eine enge Verzahnung zwischen digitalen Entwurfs- und Fertigungsprozessen ermöglicht wurde. Die Architekten kreierten einen Raum, der die Abkehr von der bisherigen Prägung durch die Postmoderne ausdrückt und einen angemessenen Rahmen für die Präsentation von Produkten einer neuen Generation von Designern und Architekten schafft.

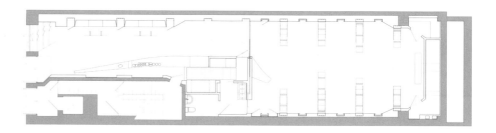

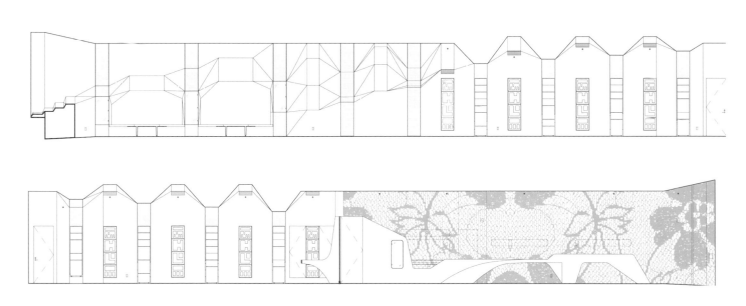

bisazza showroom | berlin . germany

D E S I G N :   Bisazza Design Studio, under the special direction of architect Carlo Dal Bianco

The shimmering glass mosaics of the Italian manufacturer are the focus of the presentation at the Berlin flagship store. Having its own representatives in the large cities of the world is an important marketing and sales instrument for the company. It now maintains six flagship stores in Berlin, Milan, London, New York, Paris, and Barcelona. In the creation of the mosaics and the interiors, the company has entered into many partnerships through the years with outstanding architects and designers such as Michael Graves, Ettore Sottsass, and Alessandro Mendini – who was also the in-house art director at times. At the Berlin showroom, which reopened after renovation in November 2005, the graphic structures and floral elements on the floors and walls are already seen from the outside through the store window. The visitor can study the expressive variety of colors and the effect of the collections on a room in the original at this site. This is advantageous because the mosaics can best develop their spatial effects on larger surfaces. The pictures and graphics are printed directly on the surface of the glass mosaic through a computer-supported process. The presentation is enhanced by opulent chandeliers and classic examples of furniture design such as the "egg" that architect Arne Jacobsen created in 1958 for the lobby in the Royal Hotel in Copenhagen.

Die schillernden Glasmosaike des italienischen Herstellers Bisazza stehen im Zentrum der Präsentation im Berliner Flagship-Store. Für das Unternehmen bilden eigene Repräsentanzen in den weltweiten Metropolen ein wichtiges Instrument im Marketing und Vertrieb. Es unterhält mittlerweile sechs Flagship-Stores in Berlin, Mailand, London, New York, Paris und Barcelona. Bei der Gestaltung der Mosaike und Interieurs wurden im Laufe der Zeit zahlreiche Partnerschaften mit herausragenden Architekten und Designern geschlossen wie beispielsweise mit Michael Graves, Ettore Sottsass sowie Alessandro Mendini, der zeitweise Artdirector des Unternehmens war. Im Berliner Showroom, der im November 2005 nach einer Renovierung neu eröffnete, sind die grafischen Strukturen und floralen Elemente an Böden und Wänden bereits von außen durch das Schaufenster sichtbar. Der Besucher kann die expressive Farbvielfalt und Raumwirkung der Kollektionen vor Ort im Original studieren. Das ist von Vorteil, da die Mosaike ihre räumliche Wirkung am besten auf größeren Flächen entfalten. Die Bilder und Grafiken werden über ein computergestütztes Verfahren direkt auf die Oberfläche der Glasmosaike aufgedruckt. Ergänzt wird die Präsentation von opulenten Lüstern und Klassikern des Möbeldesigns wie dem „Ei", das 1958 der Architekt Arne Jacobsen für die Lobby im Royal Hotel in Kopenhagen entwarf.

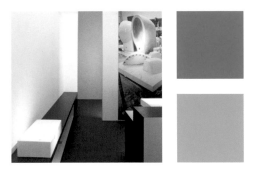

catalano | stuttgart . germany

DESIGN: no w here architekten Amann & Volpp Gbr

Ceramica Catalano opened a showroom in the direct vicinity of the new Stuttgart Art Museum in October 2005. The spacious store window alone awakens interest in the puristic sanitary objects – which are effectively staged – on the part of potential builders and customers. The clear forms characterize both the products and the overall appearance of the Italian manufacturer. The Stuttgart office of no w here architekten translated these plans into a restrained and peaceful framework for the various program series. In order to ensure the flexibility throughout the entire exhibition space, the architects accommodated all of the "service" functions in a rear area with cubes that have various formats depending on their purpose. The front presentation area displays the products like sculptures on pedestals or stacks them artistically in display cases. A dynamically formed seating arrangement invites visitors to relax as they look at the exhibition and have extended conversations. Large-scale illustrations with alienated details of the production process set accents in the presentation, which is very calm as a whole. The dark color of the synthetic-resin floor and the furnishings allow the pale ceramic products to appear in their best light.

In unmittelbarer Nähe zum neuen Stuttgarter Kunstmuseum eröffnete Ceramica Catalano im Oktober 2005 einen Showroom. Schon das großzügige Schaufenster weckt bei potentiellen Bauherren und Kunden das Interesse an den puristischen Sanitärobjekten, die effektvoll in Szene gesetzt werden. Die klaren Formen bestimmen sowohl die Produkte als auch den Gesamtauftritt des italienischen Herstellers. Das Stuttgarter Büro no w here architekten übersetzte diese Vorgaben in einen zurückhaltenden und ruhigen Rahmen für die verschiedenen Programmserien. Um Flexibilität auf der gesamten Ausstellungsfläche zu garantieren, brachten die Architekten alle „dienenden" Funktionen im rückwärtigen Bereich in Kuben unter, die je nach Funktion unterschiedliche Formate haben. Im vorderen Präsentationsbereich werden die Produkte wie Skulpturen auf Sockel gestellt oder in Vitrinen kunstvoll gestapelt. Zwischen den Objekten lädt eine dynamisch geformte Sitzlandschaft zum entspannten Betrachten der Ausstellung und zu vertiefenden Gesprächen ein. Großformatige Abbildungen mit verfremdeten Details aus der Produktion setzen Akzente in der insgesamt ruhigen Präsentation. Die dunkle Farbe des Kunstharzbodens und des Mobiliars lässt die hellen Keramikprodukte in bestem Licht erscheinen.

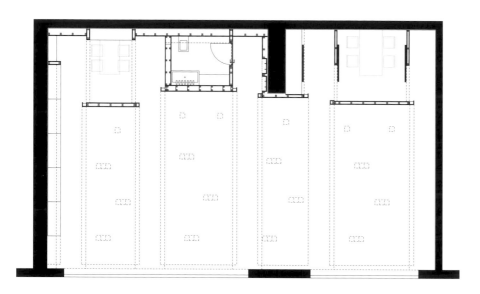

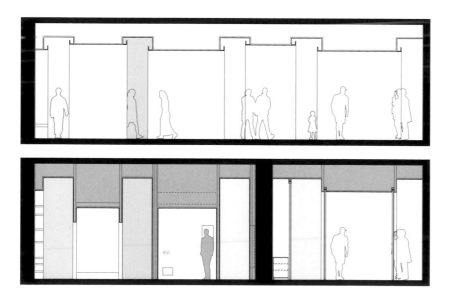

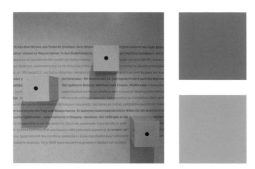

duravit design center | hornberg . germany

DESIGN: architecture: Philippe Starck; exhibition design: Atelier Brückner

The designers of the Stuttgart Atelier Brückner studio have dramatized aspects of "life in the bathroom" on the five floors of the Duravit Design Center, which opened in December 2004. The visitor comes into increasingly closer contact with the products and therefore with the Duravit company through the individual floors: from the ground floor where the products are exhibited like museum pieces in an overstated way to the 5th floor where "bathing" is allowed. The Duravit Design Center integrates uses like the showroom and a center for service, events, and training. The company's partners from trade and commerce meet here, as do architects, planners, and customers. Philippe Starck has made a humorous statement in the tranquil Black Forest with a 23-foot tall sculpture of a toilet. The ground floor of the exhibit cube presents design objects on pedestals. All of the designers who have worked for Duravit during the past decades have their biographies and projects displayed on the walls. The second floor gives the visitors an insight into the design process and production. A timeline of the Duravit company history on the third floor runs parallel to the history of architecture and design. The next levels provide product information and exhibit bathrooms, which visitors are also welcome to try out.

Die Gestalter vom Stuttgarter Atelier Brückner haben im Duravit Design Center, das im Dezember 2004 eröffnete, auf fünf Etagen Aspekte zum Thema „Leben im Bad" inszeniert. Der Besucher nähert sich den Produkten und damit der Firma Duravit über die einzelnen Etagen immer stärker an: vom Erdgeschoss, wo die Produkte überhöht, museal ausgestellt sind, bis zum 4. Obergeschoss, wo er „in ihnen baden" kann. Das Duravit Design Center fasst Nutzungen wie Showroom, Service-, Veranstaltungs- und Trainingscenter zusammen. Partner des Unternehmens aus Handel und Handwerk treffen sich hier ebenso wie Architekten, Planer und Kunden. Philippe Starck hat mit einer über sieben Meter hohen WC-Skulptur in der Fassade ein humorvolles Zeichen im beschaulichen Schwarzwald gesetzt. Im Erdgeschoss des Ausstellungskubus werden Designobjekte auf Podesten präsentiert. An den Wänden werden alle Designer, die in den vergangenen Jahrzehnten für Duravit gearbeitet haben, mit ihrer Vita und Projekten vorgestellt. Im ersten Geschoss erhält der Besucher dann einen Einblick in den Designprozess und die Produktion. In der zweiten Etage wird entlang einer Zeitachse die Firmengeschichte von Duravit parallel zur Architektur- und Designgeschichte dargestellt. Die folgenden Ebenen dienen der Produktinformation bis hin zu den Ausstellungsbädern, die auch ausprobiert werden dürfen.

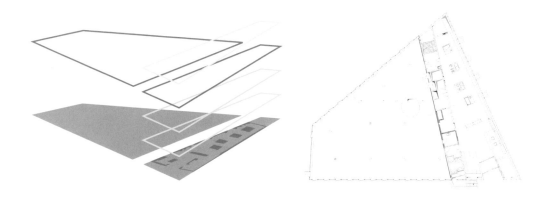

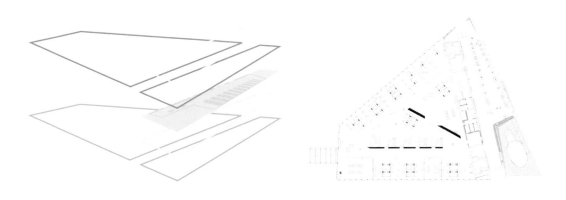

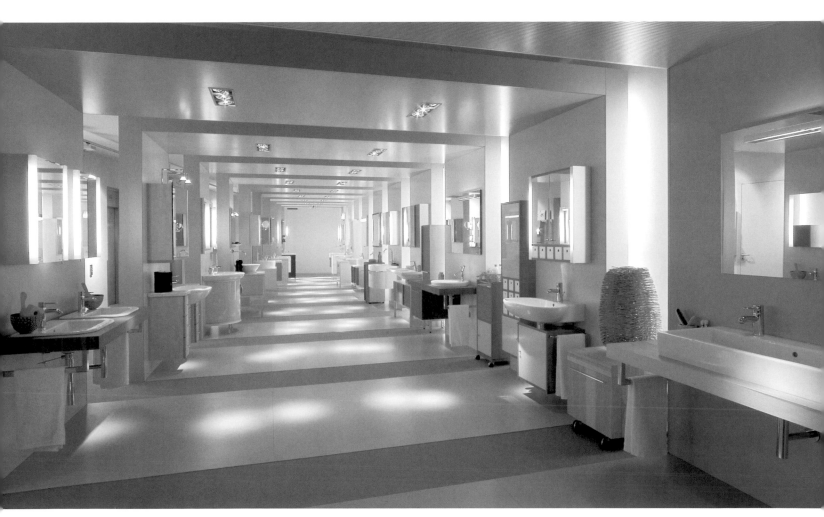

kaldewei kompetenz center | ahlen . germany

DESIGN: BOLLES+WILSON GmbH & Co. KG

The core competence of the Kaldewei company lies in the production of highquality bathtubs and shower bases that are finished with enamel that it produces. The glass-like covering, which was already known before ancient times, has been continuously developed here as a high-tech surface. The visitor to the Kaldewei Komepetenz Center experiences the meeting of red-hot fluid enamel and water as an impressive event. The tubs are manufactured in the nearby production halls. Enamel as a mark of the Kaldewei brand's quality can also be found in the façade of the Komepetenz Center, which was opened in March 2005. The architects BOLLES+WILSON have developed a structure of narrow enamel strips that run around the complex of old enamel smelter and the adjoined Komepetenz Center in the colors of the product range. The new overall form simultaneously retains the heterogeneous existing building and makes it possible to read the history of the company's nucleus. The Komepetenz Center, which also serves as a showroom and an information and training center, is accessed through the spatially staggered entrance lobby. The warm tone of its oak panels creates a cozy atmosphere. This is the invitation to experience the products up close: In separate test bathrooms, end customers who have made appointments can try out the various tubs with different whirl systems in peace and quiet.

Die Kernkompetenz des Unternehmens Kaldewei liegt in der Herstellung hochwertiger Bade- und Duschwannen, die mit Email aus eigener Produktion veredelt werden. Die schon vor der Antike bekannte glasartige Beschichtung wird hier kontinuierlich als Hightech-Oberfläche fortentwickelt. Als eindrucksvolles Ereignis erlebt der Besucher des Kaldewei Kompetenz Centers das Zusammentreffen von glühend flüssigem Email und Wasser. Die Wannen selbst werden in den nahe gelegenen Fabrikationshallen produziert. Email als Qualitätsmerkmal der Marke Kaldewei findet sich auch an der Fassade des im März 2005 eröffneten Kompetenz Centers wieder. Die Architekten BOLLES+WILSON haben eine Struktur aus schmalen Emailstreifen entwickelt, die den Komplex aus alter Emailschmelze und angebautem Kompetenz Center in den Farben der Produktpalette umspielen. Die neue Gesamtform lässt so gleichzeitig die heterogenen Bauvolumen und damit die Geschichte der Keimzelle des Unternehmens ablesbar. Das Kompetenz Center, gleichzeitig Showroom, Informations- und Schulungszentrum, wird über die räumlich gestaffelte Eingangslobby erschlossen. Der warme Ton seiner Eichenpaneele erzeugt eine behagliche Atmosphäre. Dies ist die Einladung, die Produkte hautnah zu erleben: In separaten Probebädern können Endkunden nach Voranmeldung in Ruhe unterschiedliche Wannen mit verschiedenen Whirlsystemen testen.

kvadrat sanden showroom | stockholm . sweden
DESIGN: Ronan & Erwan Bouroullec

Commercial lofts, workshops, and studios lend character to the surroundings of the new showroom for the Danish fabric manufacturer Kvadrat in Stockholm's Södermalm district. An amazing space with textile dividing walls was created on the ground floor of a former spinning mill at the beginning of 2005. The brothers Ronan and Erwan Bouroullec had received an open job specification from their client: The furnishing of an expressive showroom with the sole condition of incorporating the presentation of fabric for curtains and furnishings. "The showroom realizes lengthy considerations on how to construct rooms out of textiles", is how the French designers summarized the task. Using the material of fabric, they created flexible rooms that established a direct relationship to the company. The basic module is a fabric brick that can be linked with others through an ingenious quick-connect system. The textile "building blocks" have a core of foam and can be covered with various fabrics. This makes it possible to design walls that are both expressive and soft. The play of color ranges from cool gray and beige to bright orange and muted green and black. The light-colored floor covering of douglas fir creates a natural, calm atmosphere in harmony with the acoustically effective fabric walls.

Gewerbelofts, Werkstätten und Ateliers prägen die Umgebung des neuen Showrooms für den dänischen Stoffhersteller Kvadrat im Stockholmer Stadtteil Södermalm. Im Erdgeschoss einer ehemaligen Spinnerei ist hier Anfang 2005 ein erstaunlicher Raum mit textilen Trennwänden entstanden. Die Brüder Ronan und Erwan Bouroullec hatten von ihrem Auftraggeber ein offenes Anforderungsprofil erhalten: Die Einrichtung eines ausdrucksvollen Showrooms mit der einzigen Auflage, die Präsentation von Vorhang- und Möbelstoffen zu berücksichtigen. „Der Showroom verwirklicht langwierige Überlegungen, Räume aus Textilien zu konstruieren", fassen es die französischen Designer zusammen. Sie schufen mit dem Material Stoff flexible Räume, die einen unmittelbaren Bezug zum Unternehmen herstellen. Das Grundmodul ist ein Stoffziegel, der durch ein raffiniertes Stecksystem mit anderen verbunden werden kann. Die textilen „Bausteine" haben einen Kern aus Schaumstoff und können mit verschiedenen Stoffen bezogen werden. So ist es möglich, expressive und gleichzeitig weiche Wände zu gestalten. Das Farbenspiel reicht von kühlem Grau und Beige über kräftiges Orange bis hin zu gedämpftem Grün und Schwarz. Der helle Bodenbelag aus Douglasholz schafft im Einklang mit den akustisch wirksamen Stoffwänden eine Atmosphäre von Natürlichkeit und Ruhe.

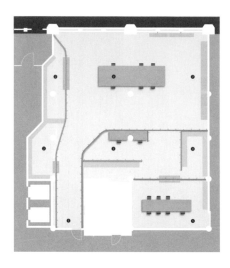

muji | milan . italy

DESIGN: studioFASE & AlivertiSamsaArchitetti

The MUJI brand was launched to stand up to the growing flood of brand-name articles. The name is a shortened form of mujirushi ryohin, the translation of which means: "no brand, good products". The guiding principles of the chain, which was founded in 1980, are influenced by aspects such as minimalist design, functionality, and a production method that conserves resources. As a result, the products such as office articles, cosmetics, and decorative accessories are sold without any visible trademarks. MUJI has now established itself as a brand that has well-known designers working for it. However, their names are not directly displayed on the products. Since 1990, a network of independent branches has developed in urban downtown locations. The store in Milan is also on a lively shopping street with small businesses full of visual appeal. The large store window consists of one single pane of glass that sets a peaceful accent in the busy Via Torino. The store is on the ground floor and lower level of narrow and winding shop premises. In order to guide the customers through it, a so-called "lightbox" with the characteristic logo of the company has been placed at the most important points of orientation. Another distinguishing element for the space is the continuous rows of shelves that showcase the assortment of products.

Die Marke MUJI wurde ins Leben gerufen, um der wachsenden Flut von Markenartikeln Paroli zu bieten. Der Name ist die Kurzform von „mujirushi ryohin", was übersetzt soviel bedeutet wie: „Keine Marke, gute Produkte". Die Leitsätze der 1980 gegründeten Handelskette sind geprägt von Aspekten wie minimalistisches Design, Funktionalität und eine Ressourcen schonende Produktionsweise. Die Produkte wie Büroartikel, Kosmetika und Wohnaccessoires werden ohne sichtbares Markenkennzeichen vertrieben. MUJI hat sich mittlerweile selbst zu einer Marke etabliert, für die bekannte Designer arbeiten, deren Namen aber nicht in direkte Erscheinung treten. Seit 1990 entwickelt sich ein Netzwerk von unabhängigen Filialen in urbanen Innenstadtlagen. Auch der Store in Mailand ist in eine lebendige Einkaufsstraße mit kleinteiligen Geschäften voller visueller Reize integriert. Das große Schaufenster besteht aus einer einzigen Glasscheibe, die einen ruhigen Akzent in der quirligen Via Torino setzt. Der Store befindet sich im Erd- und Untergeschoss eines verwinkelten Ladenlokales. Um die Kunden durch das Geschäft zu führen, wurde an den wichtigsten Orientierungspunkten eine so genannte „Lightbox" mit dem charakteristischen Logo des Unternehmens platziert. Ein weiteres raumbestimmendes Element sind die kontinuierlich durchlaufenden Regale, die das Sortiment in Szene setzen.

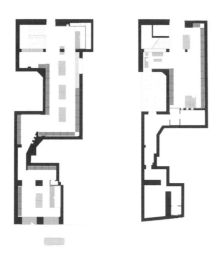

raab karcher flagship store | berlin . germany
DESIGN: franken architekten

The first flagship store of the Raab Karcher brand has been built in Berlin on the Kurfürstendamm in direct proximity to representatives of the famous fashion labels. The goal of the globally active building-materials dealer is to for private customers, developers, and architects, in addition to suppliers for the wholesale trade, to visit the new showroom. The team of franken architekten planned the flagship store for a collection from the area of tile and bathroom landscapes. The store is open to the gaze of people strolling by and holds surprises: Their eyes are led through the so-called "liquid wall," an acrylic glass pane that gives the impression of a distorting lens and causes the back wall to oscillate optically. All of the installations and furniture follow the viewer's visual rays from outside to inside. This means forgoing the right angles and leads to the effect that every single installation and piece of furniture looks unique. The interior is organized into the informal reception area, the product information, and cabinets of partner companies from the field of tile and fixtures, with which Raab Karcher presents itself in the new store. This is where the company meets the demand for an upvaluation of the private sanitary area – which is increasingly developing into a discerning retreat for relaxation and wellness.

In unmittelbarer Nähe zu den Repräsentanzen der bekanntesten Modelabels ist in Berlin am Kurfürstendamm der erste Flagship-Store der Marke Raab Karcher entstanden. Ziel des international agierenden Baustoffhändlers ist es, mit dem neuen Showroom nicht nur als Zulieferer für den Großhandel, sondern auch bei privaten Kunden, Bauherren und Architekten wahrgenommen zu werden. Das Team von franken architekten plante den Flagship-Store für eine Kollektion aus dem Bereich Fliesen- und Badelandschaften. Das Geschäft öffnet sich den Blicken des Flaneurs und überrascht ihn: Der Blick wird durch die sogenannte „liquid wall" geleitet, eine Acrylglasscheibe, die wie eine Zerrlinse wirkt und die Rückwand optisch ins Schwingen bringt. Alle Einbauten und Möbel folgen den Sehstrahlen des Betrachters von außen nach innen. Dies bedeutet den Verzicht auf rechte Winkel und führt dazu, dass alle Einbauten und Möbel Unikate sind. Der Innenraum gliedert sich in den informellen Empfang, die Produktinformation und die Kabinette der Partnerunternehmen aus dem Bereich Fliesen und Armaturen, mit denen sich Raab Karcher im neuen Geschäft gemeinsam präsentiert. Mit dem Store kommt das Unternehmen der Aufwertung der privaten Sanitärbereiche nach, die sich immer mehr zu anspruchsvollen Rückzugsorten für Entspannung und Wellness entwickeln.

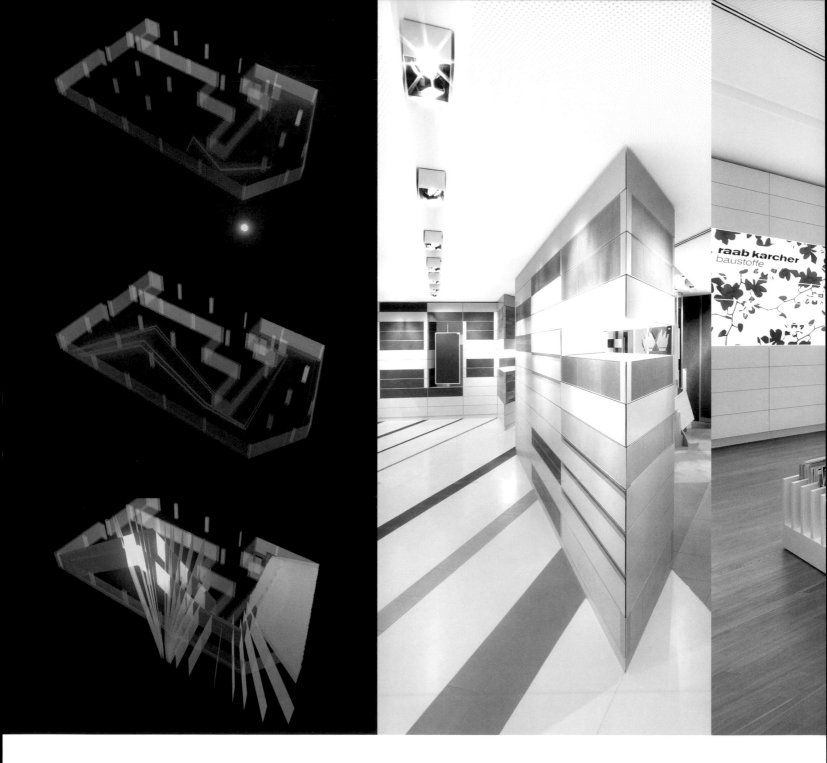

stua | paris . france
DESIGN: Jon Gasca

The filigree curtains of silk thread that help shape rooms and create moods of light are a typical element in the appearance of the Spanish furniture manufacturer Stua. The textile walls of thread are found not only at the flagship store in Paris but also at the Stua Shop in Bilbao and the numerous trade-fair presentations. The tactile appeal that radiates from the white threads practically encourages the visitor to touch them and trigger their dynamic way of swinging. The Stua Shop in Paris was completed in March 2005 and is located in a building with foundation walls dating back to the Middle Ages. Art director Jon Gasca has extensively integrated the century-old building structure into the new presentation concept. The facade remains almost unchanged, and the existing structures have been maintained for the most part in the interior of the two-story retail business. The crooked beams on the ground floor were given a black coat of paint, and they create a dramatic counterpart to the contemporary products. The vault on the lower level was merely cleaned. The furniture is presented here on white pedestals that function like a backlit box and effectively illuminate the exhibits from below. As a result, the historical framework offers an authentic and high-contrast stage for the entire Stua collection.

Ein typisches Element im Erscheinungsbild des spanischen Möbelherstellers Stua sind die filigranen Vorhänge aus Seidenfäden, mit denen Räume gebildet und Lichtstimmungen erzeugt werden. Die textilen Fadenwände finden sich nicht nur im Flagship-Store in Paris, sondern auch im Stua Shop in Bilbao und in den zahlreichen Messepräsentationen. Der taktile Reiz, der von den weißen Fäden ausgeht, fordert die Besucher geradezu auf, sie zu berühren und in dynamische Schwingungen zu versetzen. Der Stua Shop in Paris wurde im März 2005 fertiggestellt und befindet sich in einem Gebäude, dessen Grundmauern bereits aus dem Mittelalter stammen. Artdirector Jon Gasca hat die jahrhundertealte Bausubstanz weitgehend in das neue Präsentationskonzept einbezogen. Die Fassade blieb fast unverändert, und auch im Inneren des zweistöckigen Ladengeschäftes blieben die vorgefundenen Strukturen weitgehend erhalten. Die krummen Balken im Erdgeschoss wurden mit einem schwarzen Anstrich versehen und bilden einen spannungsvollen Gegenpol zu den zeitgemäßen Produkten. Das Gewölbe im Untergeschoss wurde lediglich gereinigt. Die Möbel präsentieren sich hier auf weißen Podesten, welche wie ein Leuchtkasten funktionieren und die Exponate effektvoll von unten beleuchten. Der historische Rahmen stellt so eine authentische und kontrastreiche Bühne für die gesamte Stua-Kollektion dar.

STUA

Globus
Miniature

produced for STUA by
Vitra Design Museum

STUA

STUA

STUA

STUA

STUA

one by one

steybe kindermöbelhaus | endersbach . germany
DESIGN: Fuchs, Wacker

When driving through the typical industrial parks on the outskirts of a city, we rarely find upmarket architecture that moves us to stop and find out what the business offers. Things are different in the rather tranquil Remstal valley. At the entrance to the town of Weinstadt-Endersbach, three austere structures with clear cubature and precisely carved openings pleasantly stand out from the architectural context of the neighborhood. Spacious display windows that lead around the corner of the building and extend over several levels make it possible for grown-up – and little – visitors to have a look at the exhibit. After all, this is the children's furniture store Steybe that opened here in November 2003 and was designed by the architects Fuchs, Wacker. Joints separate the cubes from each other, and each cube is different in its form, size, and use. In the interior, ramps and concrete steps connect the exhibition areas on several levels. The ceilings and walls are made of exposed concrete that has only been painted in order to create a calm background for the colorful products. A black pigmented cement stone floor underscores this effect. A large airspace opens up the view of the 20-foot high exhibition wall that presents toys and children's furniture in a way that closely resembles a museum.

Auf der Fahrt durch die typischen Gewerbegebiete der Peripherie findet man selten anspruchsvolle Architektur, die zum Anhalten bewegt, um zu erfahren, was hier wohl präsentiert wird. Anders im eher beschaulichen Remstal. Am Ortseingang von Weinstadt-Endersbach heben sich wohltuend drei strenge Baukörper mit klarer Kubatur und präzise eingeschnittenen Öffnungen vom baulichen Kontext der Nachbarschaft ab. Großzügige Schaufenster, die um die Gebäudekanten hinweg führen und über mehrere Ebenen reichen, ermöglichen großen und auch kleinen Besuchern einen Blick in die Ausstellung. Schließlich handelt es sich um das Kindermöbelhaus Steybe, das im November 2003 hier eröffnete und von Fuchs, Wacker Architekten entworfen wurde. Die Kuben sind durch Fugen voneinander getrennt und unterscheiden sich jeweils in ihrer Form, Größe und Nutzung. Im Inneren verbinden Rampen und Betonstufen die Ausstellungsflächen auf mehreren Ebenen. Die Decken und Wände bestehen aus Sichtbeton, der lediglich gestrichen wurde, um einen ruhigen Hintergrund für die farbigen Produkte zu bilden. Schwarz pigmentierter Zementestrich unterstreicht diese Wirkung. Ein großer Luftraum gibt den Blick auf die sechs Meter hohe Ausstellungswand frei, an der Spielzeuge und Kindermöbel ganz ähnlich wie in einem Museum präsentiert werden.

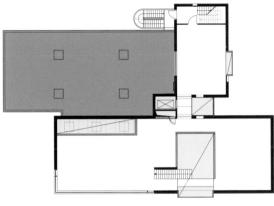

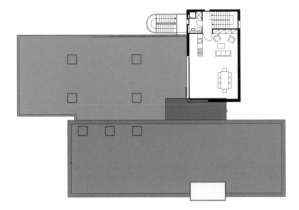

health . food

dr. oetker welt | bielefeld . germany

DESIGN: Triad Berlin, Designer: Frank Ophoff

Every future needs an origin. This basic idea extends throughout the entire staging of the Dr. Oetker brand exhibit in Bielefeld. The side brick structures of the old production hall – which is also called the "Pudding-Mixture Building" – are still standing. Since March 2005, the foyer to the exhibit that presents the brand's history opens up between them behind a bold glass wall. An exciting contrast arises at the interface between historic industrial architecture and modern exhibit scenography. The architects and designers of Triad Berlin have designed nine thematic areas that show the path from the raw material to the finished product on the set table. Pharmacist Dr. August Oetker's pioneering invention of ready-for-use packaged baking powder is the focus of the first showroom. The interactive course stretches over eight more stations with films, pictures, mini-laboratories, and original manufacturing machines. The visitor strolls between giant-sized blow-ups of packaging, listens to the voice of the founder, or enters into a kitchen filled with all sorts of good smells. Slim graphic banners with quotes from the four leading personalities of the company run like a red thread throughout the entire exhibit area.

Jede Zukunft braucht Herkunft. Dieser Grundgedanke zieht sich durch die gesamte Inszenierung der Markenausstellung von Dr. Oetker in Bielefeld. Von der alten Produktionshalle, die auch „Puddingpulverbau" genannt wird, blieben die seitlichen Backsteingebäude erhalten. Dazwischen öffnet sich seit März 2005 hinter einer kühnen Glaswand das Foyer zur Ausstellung, welche die Geschichte der Marke inszeniert. An der Schnittstelle zwischen historischer Industriearchitektur und moderner Ausstellungsszenografie entsteht ein spannungsreicher Kontrast. Die Architekten und Designer von Triad Berlin konzipierten neun Themenbereiche, die den Weg vom Rohstoff bis zum fertigen Produkt am gedeckten Tisch aufzeigen. Die bahnbrechende Erfindung des gebrauchsfertig abgepackten Backpulvers durch den Apotheker Dr. August Oetker steht im Mittelpunkt des ersten Ausstellungsraumes. Der erlebnisorientierte Parcours erstreckt sich über acht weitere Stationen mit Filmen, Bildern, Minilaboren und originalen Fertigungsmaschinen. Der Besucher flaniert zwischen Blow-Ups von Verpackungen, lauscht der Stimme des Gründers oder begibt sich in eine duftende Küche. Schmale grafische Schriftbänder mit Zitaten der vier Unternehmerpersönlichkeiten ziehen sich wie ein roter Faden durch den gesamten Ausstellungsbereich.

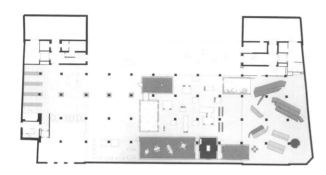

Rezeptorium

Rezepte auf Verpackungen, bis heute eine Besonderheit der Dr. Oetker-Produkte, gab es bereits in den Gründungsjahren des Unternehmens. Schon auf den ersten Backpulvertütchen fanden die Verbraucher verschiedene Rezepte zum Ausprobieren, was die Attraktivität der Produkte steigerte. Die originelle Idee des Gründers trug mit zum steilen Aufstieg des Unternehmens bei. Nicht nur auf Verpackungen, sondern auch auf Postkarten, auf Sammelkarten in Broschüren, in Anzeigen sowie in Koch- und Backbüchern – überall waren seine Rezepte zu finden. Heute hat man auch die Möglichkeit, Rezepte aus den verschiedenen Bereichen direkt aus dem Internet herunterzuladen.

Aus den kostenlosen Rezeptheftchen wurden Bücher: 1911 erschien die sogenannte 'Bibel des Kochens', das legendäre "Dr. Oetker Schulkochbuch". Bis heute ist es fester Bestandteil vieler deutscher Haushalte und wird teilweise von Generation zu Generation weitergegeben. Für die Backfreunde brachte Dr. Oetker 1930 einen weiteren Bestseller auf den Markt. 'Backen macht Freude' löste damals einen einmaligen Backboom in Deutschland aus. Beide Bücher und die erfolgreichen Koch- und Backbücher des 20. Jahrhunderts. Seit 1950 werden die Bücher von Dr. Oetker durch einen eigenen Verlag vertrieben. In verschiedenen Reihen werden die aktuellen Koch- und Backtrends vorgestellt. Das reichhaltige Angebot zu den verschiedensten Themen macht den Dr. Oetker Verlag zum bekanntesten deutschen Kochbuchverlag.

Von Beginn an trug der Dialog mit den Kunden dazu bei, dass immer mehr Rezepte und praktische Tipps gesammelt und weitergegeben wurden. Heute sorgen 15 Rezepturen dafür, dass im Dr. Oetker Verlag laufend neue Publikationen entstehen. Eine Bandbreite von modernen Rezepten bietet den Lesern die Möglichkeit, stets neue Lieblingsrezepte zu entdecken. Pflücken Sie sich Ihr Lieblingsrezept auf unsere Rezeptwiese und probieren Sie es zu Hause aus. Ob süß oder herzhaft – in der Vielfalt der Dr. Oetker Rezepte ist für jeden Geschmack etwas dabei.

merkur markt | st. poelten . austria

DESIGN: LIMIT architects

For many years, the design of supermarkets followed strict rules that almost cut out the architecture through the dominant use of color and logo. However, since the 1990s there have been new impulses for the design of innovative and aesthetically upmarket worlds of trade, particularly from Austria. The idea that even supermarkets can be an optical enhancement has been proved by the team of LIMIT architects, which designed a new appearance for the Merkur markets. The store in St. Pölten is the prototype upon which all of the subsequent supermarkets of this chain in Austria are oriented. Its design is based upon a comprehensive concept in which the colors white and green form a visual bracket between public perception and the presentation of the foods inside. A filigree projecting roof imparts a dynamic side view linking the parking spaces and the white cube. On the interior, oversized images draw attention to the selection in the so-called food worlds, providing better orientation for the customers. When selecting the surfaces, the planners placed great emphasis upon materials that communicate values such as product freshness and quality. The Merkur supermarket in St. Pölten shows that innovative design is also possible between the prevalent extremes of discount and luxury.

Das Design von Supermärkten folgte lange Zeit straffen Regeln, welche die Architektur durch den dominanten Einsatz von Farbe und Logo fast ausblendeten. Vor allem aus Österreich kommen aber seit Anfang der 90er Jahre neue Impulse zur Gestaltung innovativer und ästhetisch anspruchsvoller Handelswelten. Dass auch Supermärkte eine optische Bereicherung sein können, beweist das Team LIMIT architects, das ein neues Erscheinungsbild für die Merkur Märkte konzipierte. Das Geschäft in St. Pölten ist der Prototyp, an dem sich alle weiteren Supermärkte in Österreich orientieren. Der Gestaltung liegt ein ganzheitliches Konzept zugrunde, bei dem die Farben Weiß und Grün eine visuelle Klammer zwischen der öffentlichen Wahrnehmung und der Präsentation der Lebensmittel im Inneren bilden. Ein filigranes Vordach vermittelt zwischen den Parkmöglichkeiten und dem weißen Kubus mit einer dynamischen Seitenansicht. Im Inneren verweisen übergroße Bilder auf das Angebot in den so genannten Food-Welten und dienen damit der besseren Orientierung für die Kunden. Bei der Auswahl der Oberflächen legten die Planer Wert auf Materialien, die Werte wie Frische und Qualität der Produkte kommunizieren. Der Merkur Markt in St. Pölten zeigt, dass innovative Gestaltung auch zwischen den verbreiteten Extremen von Discount und Luxus möglich ist.

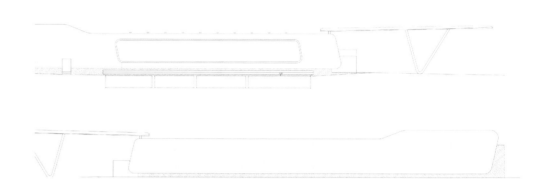

nivea haus | hamburg . germany

DESIGN: Klaus Martin Hoffmann, ECE Projektmanagement

The Beiersdorf AG company opened a new world of well-being for body, mind, and soul in April 2006 directly on the bustling Jungfernstieg street in the best location of Hamburg. The Nivea House adds a new spatial dimension to the trend of short-time wellness treatments in a comfortable day spa. On a total of three levels, the visitor will find a multitude of products and applications related to the Hanseatic brand, which now has a tradition that goes back almost 100 years. Above all, the characteristic blue crème jars are now one of the classics of packaging design. The architects of the Hamburger ECE Projektmanagement have staged a brand world on about 2,600 square feet with a mixed use of sales and wellness areas. The interior is dominated by the typical company colors of blue and white, which are firmly rooted in the tradition of the brand. Large-scale motifs explore themes on the three levels of beach, ocean, and sky. The selection of materials and the furnishings support the vacation mood and radiate a pleasantly fresh atmosphere. The builder sees the costs for the building as a new dimension of brand staging and as an investment in the value of the brand. With sustainable success, the company is considering additional locations for new flagship stores in other large cities.

In bester Lage von Hamburg eröffnete die Beiersdorf AG im April 2006 direkt am belebten Jungfernstieg eine neue Welt des Wohlbefindens für Körper, Geist und Seele. Das Nivea Haus gibt dem Trend zur Kurzzeit-Wellness im komfortablen Day-Spa eine neue räumliche Dimension. Auf insgesamt drei Ebenen findet der Besucher eine Vielzahl von Produkten und Anwendungen rund um die hanseatische Marke, die mittlerweile auf eine fast 100-jährige Tradition zurückblickt. Vor allem die charakteristischen blauen Cremedosen gehören heute zu den Klassikern des Verpackungsdesign. Die Architekten des Hamburger ECE Projektmanagement inszenierten auf rund 800 Quadratmetern eine Markenwelt mit einer Mischnutzung aus Verkaufs- und Wellness-Bereichen. Im Inneren dominieren die typischen Hausfarben Blau und Weiß, die fest in der Tradition der Marke verwurzelt sind. Großformatige Motive thematisieren auf den drei Ebenen Strand, Meer und Himmel. Die Auswahl der Materialien und des Mobiliars unterstützt die Urlaubsstimmung und verbreitet eine angenehm frische Atmosphäre. Die Kosten für das Haus versteht der Bauherr als neue Dimension der Markeninszenierung und als Investition in den Markenwert. Bei nachhaltigem Erfolg denkt das Unternehmen über weitere Standorte für neue Flagship-Stores in anderen Metropolen nach.

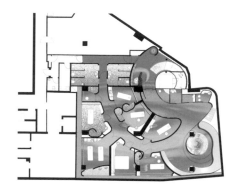

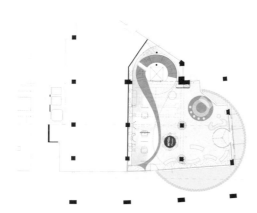

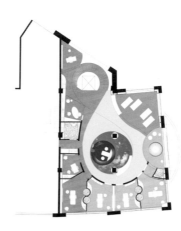

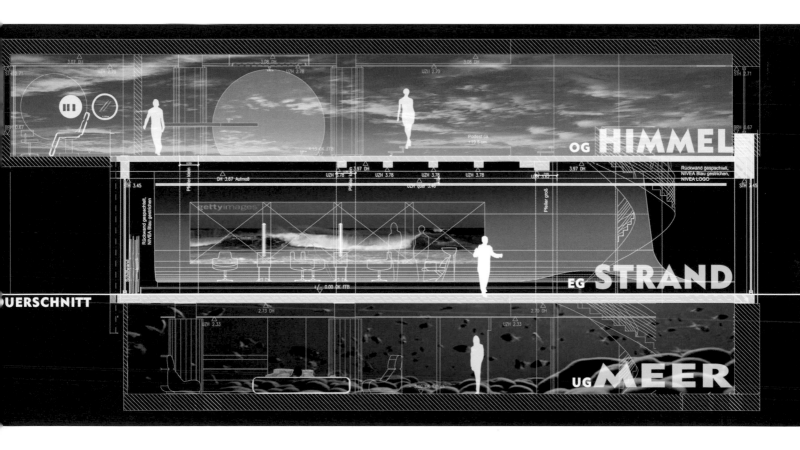

OG HIMMEL

EG STRAND

UG MEER

QUERSCHNITT

service . communication

a1 lounge | vienna . austria
DESIGN: EOOS

How do you sell virtual products such as ring tones, computer games, or contracts for the use of communication networks? Quite simply: with clouds, light, and technology. This is what the designers of EOOS from Vienna claim – and they prove it. They created a new shopping experience for the Austrian mobile service provider A1. The customers must first walk through a facade with artificial fog to reach the futuristic "new world" of communication. The fog between the layers of the 26-foot high glass facade can be condensed into various scenarios with differing transparency by means of a computer control system. Once inside, the visitor finds tables with LCD displays that offer the initial overview of the products. A so-called "ghost cellphone" – a crystalline body as large as a cellphone that stores all of the merchandise virtually – serves as the shopping basket. The customer receives the real products at the end from the check-out. The homogeneous white salesroom on the lower level is hermetically sealed from the outside world. Shopping is done here on monitors that are only connected with the room by an electronic umbilical cord. Spherical sounds intensify the futuristic impression. The "Ramp into the Future" leads the visitor to the upper floor, which has the lounge with its monolithic white bar.

Wie verkauft man virtuelle Produkte wie Klingeltöne, Computerspiele oder Verträge zur Nutzung von Kommunikationsnetzen? Ganz einfach: mit Wolken, Licht und Technologie, so behaupten und beweisen es die Designer von EOOS aus Wien. Sie entwarfen ein neues Einkaufserlebnis für den österreichischen Mobilfunkanbieter A1. Die Kunden müssen erst eine Fassade mit künstlichem Nebel durchschreiten, um in die futuristische „Neue Welt" der Kommunikation zu gelangen. Der Nebel zwischen den Schichten der acht Meter hohen Glasfassade kann über eine Computersteuerung zu verschiedenen Szenarien mit unterschiedlicher Transparenz verdichtet werden. Im Inneren trifft der Besucher auf Tische aus LCD-Displays, die einen ersten Überblick zu den Produkten bereit halten. Als Einkaufskorb dient ein so genanntes „Ghost-Mobiltelefon", ein kristalliner Körper von der Größe eines Handys, der alle Waren virtuell erfasst. Die realen Produkte erhält der Kunde schließlich an der Kasse. Der homogen weiße Verkaufsraum im Untergeschoss ist hermetisch von der Außenwelt abgeschlossen. Eingekauft wird hier an Bildschirmen, die nur über eine elektronische Nabelschnur mit dem Raum verbunden sind. Sphärische Klänge verstärken den futuristischen Eindruck, während man über die „Zukunfts-Rampe" in das Obergeschoss gelangt, in der sich die Lounge mit der monolithisch weißen Bar befindet.

a1 lounge

a1 lounge

og bar
     conference

eg news

ug shop

hilti brand world 2006 | schaan . liechtenstein

DESIGN : Triad Berlin, Designer: Ulf Eberspächer

The Hilti Aktiengesellschaft supplies the international building industry with products, systems, and services that are leaders in the field of technology. For the new training center in Liechtenstein, Triad Berlin designed and realized an exhibition area of more than 3,200 square feet on two floors. The tour begins on the first floor with the portrayal of important segments from the company's history. Its development is not treated historically but illuminated on the basis of selected areas: the Hilti family, development of the markets, product range, the Hilti brand, and the typical Hilti case. Above all, the Hilti Brand World is concerned with the philosophy of the Hilti brand. Its focus is on the people who work with and for Hilti. The design of the individual exhibits incorporates the materials of concrete, steel, and wood (MDF) because the company develops equipment and technology for their processing. There are absolutely no facings or veneer – everything is authentic. Like the products themselves, the operation of the exhibits has been designed in a very ergonomic way. The color red establishes a clear relationship with the brand. As a result, the exhibition is primarily oriented toward the products and their qualities. It creates a clearly recognizable brand environment in order to delve into the philosophy behind the products.

Die Hilti Aktiengesellschaft beliefert die Bauindustrie weltweit mit technologisch führenden Produkten, Systemen und Dienstleistungen. Für das neue Trainingszentrum in Liechtenstein entwickelte und realisierte Triad Berlin eine Ausstellung mit ca. 1 000 Quadratmetern auf zwei Etagen. Der Rundgang beginnt im Erdgeschoss mit der Darstellung wichtiger Ausschnitte aus der Firmengeschichte, die jedoch nicht historisch abgehandelt wird. Die Entwicklung wird anhand ausgewählter Bereiche beleuchtet: die Familie Hilti, Entwicklung der Märkte, die Produktpalette, die Marke Hilti oder der typische Hilti-Koffer. Die Hilti Brand World beschäftigt sich vor allem mit der Philosophie der Marke Hilti. Im Mittelpunkt stehen die Menschen, die mit und für Hilti arbeiten. Die Gestaltung der Exponate ist geprägt durch die Materialien Beton, Stahl und Holz (MDF) für deren Bearbeitung das Unternehmen Geräte und Technologien entwickelt. Es gibt keinerlei Verblendungen oder Furniere, alles ist authentisch. Die Bedienung der Exponate ist analog zu den Produkten besonders ergonomisch gestaltet. Mit der Farbe Rot wird ein klarer Bezug zur Marke hergestellt. Die Ausstellung orientiert sich damit vor allem an den Produkten und ihren Qualitäten. Sie schafft einen klar erkennbaren Markenraum um sich mit der hinter den Produkten stehenden Philosophie zu beschäftigen.

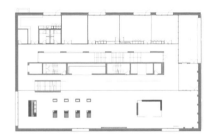

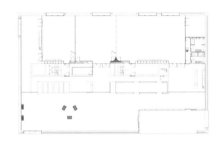

Forschung und Entwicklung
Research and Development

Wie wird ein Gerät leichter und zugleich leistungsfähiger? Die internationalen und interdisziplinären Hilti-Entwicklungsteams lösen diese und noch schwierigere Fragen. Sie bauen auf modernste Technologie und bewegen sich in einem Netzwerk, das sie mit den weltbesten Universitäten verbindet. Daraus – und aus dem einzigartigen Anwendungswissen von Hilti – entstehen Spitzenprodukte, welche die Erwartungen der Kunden nicht nur erfüllen, sondern übertreffen.

How can a tool be designed to be more powerful yet lighter? The international and interdisciplinary development teams at Hilti solve this and other even more difficult questions. They base their decisions on the most modern technology available and move in a network that links them with the best universities in the world. This combined with Hilti's unique application knowledge is the basis for top products that not only meet, but exceed customer expectations.

firmenzentrale karstadtquelle ag | essen . germany

DESIGN: Triad Berlin, Designer: Stephan Maus

The reorientation of KarstadtQuelle AG as an international department-store, tourism, and mail-order business group has not only changed the intercompany business but also the company headquarters. From the signage in the exterior and interior area to the main entrance and executive suite, the public zones on almost 10,000 square feet were revamped according to the corporate design. The centerpiece of the architectural redesign is a glass communication band that stretches from the lobby to all of the floors and the executive suite, providing a transparent and open culture of communication. Simultaneously, the communication band is the platform for an interactive brand exhibition that makes it possible to emotionally experience the history, identity, competence, locations, products, and services of KarstadtQuelle. Numerous exhibits and media presentations provide employees and visitors with an informative and entertaining insight into the world of department-store culture, tourism, and the mail-order business. The central media installation – the interactive brand showcase – communicates the expertise, people, networks, and visions of the KarstadtQuelle AG through the interplay of analog and multimedia components.

Die Neuausrichtung der KarstadtQuelle AG als internationaler Warenhaus-, Tourismus- und Versandhandelskonzern hat nicht nur das Konzerngeschäft, sondern auch die Firmenzentrale verändert. Vom Leitsystem im Außen- und Innenbereich über den Haupteingang bis zur Vorstandsetage wurden auf 3000 Quadratmetern sämtliche Publikumszonen dem Corporate Design entsprechend neu gestaltet. Das Kernstück der architektonischen Neugestaltung ist ein gläsernes Kommunikationsband, das sich vom Foyer über alle Stockwerke bis zur Vorstandsetage erstreckt und für eine transparente und offene Kommunikationskultur steht. Das Kommunikationsband ist gleichzeitig die Plattform für eine interaktive Markenausstellung, die Geschichte, Identität, Kompetenzen, Standorte, Produkte und Leistungen von KarstadtQuelle emotional erlebbar macht. Zahlreiche Exponate und mediale Inszenierungen, eröffnen Mitarbeitern und Besuchern einen ebenso informativen wie unterhaltsamen Einblick in die Welt von Warenhauskultur, Tourismus und Versandhandel. In der zentralen Medien-Installation, dem interaktiven so genannten Marken-Schaufenster, werden durch das Zusammenspiel analoger und multimedialer Komponenten Kompetenzen, Menschen, Netzwerke und Visionen der Karstadt-Quelle AG kommuniziert.

O2 flagshipstore | munich . germany
DESIGN: dan pearlman markenarchitektur gmbh

"O2 can do" is the motto of the provider of services and products associated with communication technology. The flagship store in Munich at the interface between the company and the public demonstrates what O2 does for its customers in concrete terms. The planners of Dan Pearlman from Berlin have designed an interior in which O2 presents the entire product world of the brand. This makes it possible for visitors to use an interactive media tape to receive information about rapid changes in communications technology or listen to the in-house music portal through the music browser, a jumbo headphone. The dominant element of the corporate design is unmistakably the color blue, which conveys associations of freshness and air and relates to the logo. Consequently, the entire interior and the installations are structured through shades of blue. Horizontal bands in pale shades of the company color run around the salesroom and in the service area situated on the lower level. The element of water is added here, providing refreshment to customers at a water bar. Deep-pile carpet and low seating elements with pillows exude a relaxed lounge atmosphere. At the same time, it is possible to try out equipment or watch the latest news on the shop TV.

„O2 can do" ist das Motto des Anbieters von Serviceleistungen und Produkten rund um die Kommunikationstechnik. Was O2 konkret für seine Kunden unternimmt, zeigt der Flagship-Store in München an der Schnittstelle zwischen Unternehmen und Öffentlichkeit. Die Planer von Dan Pearlman aus Berlin haben einen Innenraum gestaltet, in dem O2 die gesamte Produktwelt der Marke präsentiert. So können sich die Besucher anhand eines interaktiven Medienbandes über die rasanten Veränderungen in der Kommunikationstechnologie informieren oder über den so genannten „Music Browser", einen überdimensionalen Kopfhörer, dem hauseigenen Musikportal lauschen. Das dominante Element des Corporate Designs ist unverkennbar die Farbe Blau, die Assoziationen zu Frische und Luft vermittelt und Bezug auf das Logo nimmt. Der gesamte Innenraum und die Einbauten werden demzufolge durch Blautöne strukturiert. Horizontale Bänder in zarten Abstufungen der Hausfarbe umlaufen den Verkaufsraum und den im Untergeschoss gelegenen Servicebereich. Hier kommt noch das Element Wasser hinzu, mit dem sich die Kunden an einer Wasserbar erfrischen können. Der hochflorige Teppich und niedrige Sitzelemente mit Kissen verströmen eine entspannte Lounge-Atmosphäre. Parallel bietet sich die Möglichkeit, Geräte auszuprobieren oder sich aktuelle News im Shop-TV anzusehen.

RWE kundencenter | essen . germany

DESIGN: D'ART Design Gruppe

Room modules in the form of "energy cells" visually sum up the regional energy provider RWE Rhein-Ruhr AG's core business of energy, water, and service. On-site personal consultation is one of the company's most important communication instruments. D'ART Design Gruppe developed ring-shaped segments with different colors, materials, and functions for the new customer center. Each element simultaneously forms the floor, wall, and ceiling and is implanted in the room like a three-dimensional frame. Through the addition of the individual segment, this results in a "room within a room" that has various uses such as presentations, consultation, and online service. The individual rings pick up the lighting in order to create various moods within the interior. All elements of the furnishings – such as the information counters, displays, and shelves – are directly integrated into the room module. The first customer-service station opened in January 2002 in Essen and serves as a model for many other locations. With the flexible modules, it is possible to respond to heterogeneous space situations – even in an existing building. While creating the customer center, the designers produced a guide for design and service as informative but binding instructions for building additional customer centers.

Raummodule in Form von „Energiezellen" fassen das Kerngeschäft Energie, Wasser und Service des regionalen Energieanbieters RWE Rhein-Ruhr AG bildhaft zusammen. Die persönliche Beratung vor Ort ist eines der wichtigsten Kommunikationsinstrumente des Unternehmens. Die D'ART Design Gruppe entwickelte für die neuen Kundencenter ringförmige Segmente, die sich in Farbe, Material und Funktion unterscheiden. Jedes Element bildet gleichzeitig Boden, Wand und Decke und wird wie ein dreidimensionaler Rahmen in den Raum implantiert. Durch die Addition einzelner Segmente ergibt sich ein „Raum im Raum" mit unterschiedlichen Nutzungen wie Präsentation, Beratung und Online-Service. Einzelne Ringe nehmen die Beleuchtung auf, um verschiedene Lichtstimmungen im Innenraum zu erzeugen. Alle Elemente der Möblierung wie Informationstresen, Displays und Regale sind direkt in die Raummodule integriert. Die erste Kundenservice Station eröffnete im Januar 2002 in Essen und dient als Modell für zahlreiche weitere Standorte. Mit den flexiblen Modulen kann auf heterogene Raumsituationen, auch im Bestand, reagiert werden. Zur Realisierung der Kundencenter gestalteten die Designer einen Leitfaden für Design und Service als informative aber auch bindende Richtlinie zur Realisierung der weiteren Kundencenter.

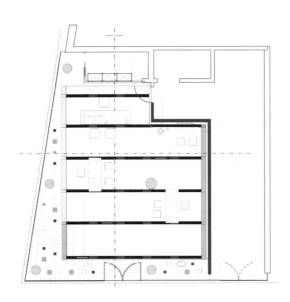

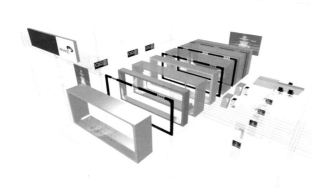

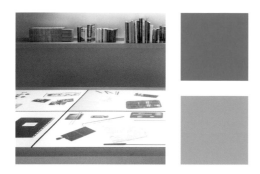

deutsche telekom ag / t-online futurezone | darmstadt . germany

DESIGN: Atelier Markgraph mit janglednerves

How do you show the future? Enabling the people of today to interactively experience the products, services, and technologies of tomorrow is the goal of the "future zone" in the Darmstadt T-Online head office. Lars Uwe Bleher of the Atelier Markgraph studio and Thomas Hundt of the multimedia agency janglednerves staged a "built image film" that leads through the development of online communication in three acts. In the first room, a turntable is set into the floor and automatically rotates the audience into the screening of a film. The visitor receives a time-lapse insight into the company's history, the start of screen text (BTX for short), and the era of the broadband boom. A curtain moving in the opposite direction serves as the projection surface and slowly transforms the room into a surround cinema. At the end of the film screening, the visitor steps through a sluice that has the effect of a "walkable browser." In the second room, the online provider's three main thematic areas are in the foreground: "Mobile Access" portrays use of the internet while en route, "Lean Forward" shows the home office, and "Lean Back" explores private internet applications. Presentations like an interactive table that allows the visitor to call up media sequences through touch illustrate the respective subject areas and actively integrate the visitor into the scenario.

Wie zeigt man Zukunft? Produkte, Dienstleistungen und Technologien von morgen für das Publikum von heute interaktiv erlebbar zu machen, ist das Ziel der „futurezone" in der Darmstädter T-Online-Zentrale. Lars Uwe Bleher vom Atelier Markgraph und Thomas Hundt von der Multimedia-Agentur janglednerves inszenierten einen „gebauten Imagefilm", der in drei Akten durch die Entwicklung der Online-Kommunikation führt. Im ersten Raum ist im Boden eine Drehscheibe eingelassen, die das Publikum automatisch in eine Filmvorführung rotiert. Hier erhält der Besucher im Zeitraffer Einblick in die Unternehmensgeschichte, vom Start des Bildschirmtextes, kurz BTX, bis hin zum Breitbandboom. Als Projektionsfläche dient ein Vorhang, der sich in entgegengesetzter Richtung bewegt und den Raum langsam in ein Rundum-Kino verwandelt. Am Ende der Filmvorführung durchschreitet der Besucher eine Schleuse, die wie ein „begehbarer Browser" wirkt. Im zweiten Raum stehen dann die drei zentralen Themenbereiche des Online-Anbieters im Vordergrund: „Mobile Access" steht für die Internetnutzung unterwegs, „Lean Forward" für das Home Office und „Lean Back" für die private Internetnutzung. Inszenierungen wie ein interaktiver Tisch, auf dem der Besucher durch Berührung Mediensequenzen abrufen kann, verdeutlichen die jeweiligen Themenbereiche und binden den Besucher aktiv in das Szenario ein.

"Nichts auf der Welt ist so mächtig, wie eine Idee, deren Zeit gekommen ist."

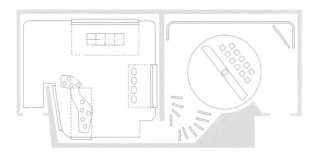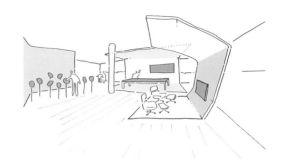

zumtobel lichtforum | dornbirn . austria

DESIGN: Herbert Resch, Zumtobel Lighting GmbH; Aysil Sari, SUPERSYMETRICS

Comprehensive light solutions are the main field of activity for the Austrian company Zumtobel Lighting GmbH. The close interplay of light and architecture characterizes the new Light Forum in the internal central warehouse at the company headquarters in Dornbirn. Aysil Sari and Herbert Resch have integrated the core expertise of "light" into the everyday working environment of the employees and customers in a vivid way. The effect of light in a space already surprises the visitor at the connecting passage to the new building. Detectors control an interactive sequence in which every movement in the homogenous white room is translated into light. The monolithic staircase leads into the connecting showroom. The lighted ceiling is controlled analogous to the daylight and sometimes allows the blue-lit stairs to subjectively appear paler at times and darker at others. This results in exciting views and light progressions that convincingly illustrate the interplay of light and architectural space. Next, the exhibition area offers a sequence of rooms on themes such as Industry & Technology, Office & Communication, Presentation & Retail, and Art & Culture. The individual cubes show concrete light solutions that convey to the visitor the direct relationship to the practice, as well as the sensual and emotional effect of light in a room.

Ganzheitliche Lichtlösungen sind das zentrale Arbeitsfeld des österreichischen Unternehmens Zumtobel Lighting GmbH. Das enge Zusammenspiel von Licht und Architektur prägt das neue Lichtforum im internen Zentrallager am Stammsitz in Dornbirn. Aysil Sari und Herbert Resch integrierten die Kernkompetenz „Licht" anschaulich in das alltägliche Arbeitsumfeld der Mitarbeiter und der Kunden. Schon im Verbindungsgang zum Neubau überrascht die Wirkung von Licht im Raum den Besucher: Bewegungsmelder steuern eine interaktive Sequenz, in der alle Bewegungen in dem homogen weißen Raum in Licht umgesetzt werden. Der monolithische Treppenraum leitet in den anschließenden Ausstellungsraum. Die Lichtdecke wird analog zum Tageslicht gesteuert und lässt die blau erleuchteten Treppenstufen subjektiv mal heller und mal dunkler erscheinen. So ergeben sich spannende Durchblicke und Lichtverläufe, die das Zusammenspiel von Licht und architektonischem Raum überzeugend veranschaulichen. Im Ausstellungsbereich folgt eine Passage entlang von Raumsequenzen zu Themen wie beispielsweise Industrie & Technik, Büro & Kommunikation, Präsentation & Verkauf und Kunst & Kultur. In den einzelnen Kuben werden konkrete Lichtlösungen gezeigt, die dem Besucher den unmittelbaren Praxisbezug sowie die sinnliche und emotionale Wirkung von Licht im Raum vermitteln.

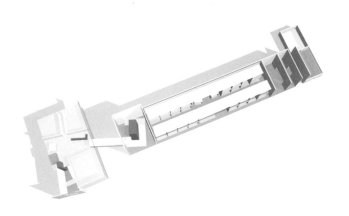

index & photo credits

imprint

Bibliographic Information published by Die Deutsche Bibliothek
Die Deutsche Bibliothek lists this publication in the Deutsche
Nationalbibliografie; detailed bibliographic data are available in the
internet at http://dnb.ddb.de

ISBN 13: 978-3-89986-083-2

1st edition

Printed in Austria

Editor | Jons Messedat
Editorial Coordination | Hanna Martin, Patricia Massó, Manuela Roth
Texts | Jons Messedat
Translations | Alphagriese.de

Layout | Anne Dörte Schmidt
Digital Imaging | Jan Hausberg
Printing | Vorarlberger Verlagsanstalt AG, Dornbirn, Austria

avedition GmbH
Königsallee 57 | 71638 Ludwigsburg | Germany
p +49-7141-1477391 | f +49-7141-1477399
www.avedition.com | contact@avedition.com

Dr. Jons Messedat
Architect & Industrial Designer
1965 born in Cologne. Heads
the Institute for Corporate
Architecture in Stuttgart and
is the author of numerous
publications on corporate
architecture and new brand
worlds. After a teaching
and research position at the
Bauhaus-University in Weimar
he lectures at universities
in Germany and abroad.
www.messedat.com

best designed hotels:
Asia Pacific
Americas
Europe I (urban)
Europe II (countryside)
Swiss Hotels
Hotel Pools
Honeymoon Hotels
Beach Hotels
Ecological Hotels
Affordable Hotels

best designed wellness hotels:
Asia Pacific
Americas
Europe
Africa & Middle East

All books are released in
German and English